STRIPPERS STARS & PRESIDENTS

Rita Zenzen Heck

ISBN: 978-0-615-24890-5
Library of Congress Control Number: 2008907802

INTRODUCTION

Strippers, Stars & Presidents came to mind as I reflected on the many celebrities I had worked with throughout the years and began reading of their passing. I suddenly got the urge to go through the scrapbooks my mother had saved for many years and gave to me before she died. The celebrities that I had worked with as a teenage reporter to the near-present were fading away. I wanted them to be remembered.

As I looked over the photos and articles, I remembered little anecdotes about each of the subjects. Some amusing, some revealing, but all meant to honor, not to disrespect or make fun of them. Once I began writing, I wondered what happened to these people after I had worked with them. So I researched as many as I could to follow up on their current status.

While I was compiling the material, some of my most treasured subjects passed away which encouraged me to continue the research. Strippers are not a major part of this book, nor are presidents; and not all "stars" were performers. Artists, statesmen and other professionals

I encountered over the years are also "stars" in their own right and I wanted to include them, also.

Bringing this book to conclusion was the most difficult task of all. Just when I thought it was complete, an important detail would turn up like another death, a previously unknown incident or a link which seemed to demand to be included. Finally, I just gave up and said...

THIS IS THE END!

CONTENTS

CHAPTER 1

First Stars

The first-born of Marie Reiser (born on 29th & Canal in old Chicago) and Nicholas John Zenzen (born in the coal mining town of Toluca, Illinois about 60 miles south of Chicago) Rita Mae Zenzen began life as a chubby, curly black haired baby who grew to be a shy child with over tanned skin and slanty eyes making her the object of some really bad racial slurs, like the *n-----r* word and chink, the major minorities of our old south side neighborhood.

Naturally, I was devastated, but my Mom was proud of me and was always there to protect me. "I'm the n----'s/chink's mother, did you have something to say?" she'd shout in their face as we passed 2K's ice cream parlor. Nobody ever said "nothin"!

My first "star" recollection was at about age four when my mother, who had really been star struck her whole life and had great aspirations for me, asked me to tell the local butcher who our favorite movie star was. At first, I didn't respond, but finally she coaxed me into it... "Mary Fartfart!" I blurted out. (Translated...Mary Pickford.) I brought down the house!

At about seven, still overweight and teased by fellow classmates, I excelled in one thing -- writing. The Franciscan nuns at Sacred Heart Grammar School on the South Side of Chicago would put up pictures on the wall and we (the students) were to write a story about them. Mine always won the prized holy card.

Then we moved to a middle class neighborhood, still on the South Side. St. Sabina was my school there. The nuns were of the Irish Dominican order, far less demanding than the strict German Franciscans. That's when I became aware of *stars* and began collecting movie star pictures from magazines and newspapers, pasting favorites in scrap books, trading them with other neighborhood kids and writing little stories about them. The most avid trader was Ray Harrington, who lived across the street. His favorite was Fay Bainter, and he would yell loud and clear FAY BAINTER when he wanted to trade for a picture of her. Ray had an exceptionally large mouth. The story goes that he once put a fire cracker in his mouth and it went off. Who knows for sure?

Another neighbor, **Norm "Hots" Michaels** whose dad was a professional piano player and wrote songs with his partner, Lindsay McPhail. *Sans,* one of their best known ditties, was recorded on Mercury by "Tiny" Hill and was featured in the Ziegfeld Follies and the George White Scandals movies depicting the roarin' twenties. "Hots" toured the midwest in the 40s and 50s.

Many years later, I caught up with him at Hugh Hefner's Playboy Club in Chicago where he was the featured *first floor* entertainment. He was also responsible for introducing me to the entertainment world first hand in my early teen years – a job with a theatrical booking agency.

Then there was my elementary schoolmate, Julie Christie who was related to jazz singer June Christie. We were so impressed. My Mom also took me to see the Major Boze amateur hour, Quiz Kids, WLS Barn Dance and Topsy and Eva, the Dunkin (nicknamed the Drunken) Sisters.

During my fourteenth summer vacation, before entering Calumet high School on the south side of Chicago, I got a job at Woolworth's (five and dime store) in downtown Chicago, teaching knitting (which I didn't know how to do) in the art goods department.

They had a sixteen year age requirement, and since I was only fourteen, I changed my Baptismal certificate, which the personnel office accepted. This was a switch, because when I was ten, I looked so old that we had to get a special note from the transit company to allow me to ride the street car for half fare. Now I needed to look older. It was what I did on my summer vacation.

It was truly exciting taking two street cars and the elevated every day from my far south side home to downtown Chicago, where I had never been before. I got to know the conductors pretty well, too. Because I had motion sickness. It began when I was about four and sitting on my Dad's lap on a train trip to Toluca, Illinois. I heaved in his brand new straw hat. He just shook his head, opened the window and that was the last of that hat. I threw up every day on the way to work for the first couple of weeks, so I was assigned to the door at the rear of the car. Needless to say, fellow passengers avoided me.

After summer vacation, I started life as a high school freshman at Calumet High and decided to take my writing to a new level. Though shy by nature, I mustered up enough courage to walk into our community newspaper office, the Auburn Parker, owned by South Side icon Jim Dwyer, and ask for a job. Editor Norm Woyner was friendly and agreed to give me a chance by assigning me to write *The Shadow,* a gossip column based on letters from neighborhood teens. I always started each column with an original poem which my mother saved. I still have a few of them. No one was supposed to know who the *Shadow* was. Covering the *Police Blotter* (neighborhood petty crimes and family disputes that made it to the police station) and the obituaries were my other regular assignments.

I was just fourteen and there was no pay, so I transferred to a neighborhood Woolworth's and later Spiegel's catalog billing department, a teen age sweat shop, to earn spending money. I was the fastest, most inaccurate biller they ever had. As I sent my calculator devised statements with the package down the chute, the one before would be returned on the other side to be corrected. Figures have never been one of my strong points.

When school started, I earned a little extra cash by making flowered headbands with my Grandma Reiser which, believe it or not, many brides and bridesmaids ordered for their ceremonies. Gram Reiser was a tall stately German lady from Wisconsin with tremendous wisdom and self confidence, an amazing sewing talent and the desire to be noticed. A *star* affliction, I think.

Newspaper duties were confined to after school and work hours and although no pay was involved, there were other other attractive perks: free tickets to movie previews and other events and a chance to interview the *stars*. When it came to setting up interviews, I lost my shyness and went for it!

Mel Torme was my first really *star interview*, who turned out to be a South Side neighbor. Known as the "velvet fog" because of his smooth singing style, he was appearing at the State & Lake Theatre in downtown Chicago. I arranged to meet him back stage after one of his shows. At 22 the youngest member of ASCAP (songwriters' guild), he had earned enough money from songwriting and performing to retire by the time he was thirteen. But that was before he discovered marriage...and divorce...and ALIMONY.

Performing since he was four, Torme worked as a child actor on radio, and began writing songs in his early teens. He quit Hyde Park high school to be a singer, drummer and part-time arranger with Chico Marx's band (one of the Marx brothers).

Because he was a South Side neighbor (Hyde Park), he invited me to visit him and his friends. I took him up on his offer and had my first sip of champagne at his house (only a small sip!). It was really a blast watching him play the Christmas Song, which he had just composed, and meeting his friends.

I didn't see much of Mel Torme after he married (and married) and moved away, but I kept up with him through his sister, Myrna. And I followed his amazing career in the news. His first movie was *Good News* with June Allyson and Peter Lawford. Multi-talented, Torme played the drums, acted in movies and television, performed as a singer of everything from ballads to jazz and wrote over 300 songs including the classic *Christmas Song* (chestnuts roasting on an open fire). Torme died June 5, 1999 in Los Angeles, California.

Starting high school, I had thinned down quite a bit and my mother thought I should be a model. She sent my photo to Patricia Stevens School of Modeling and, of course, they wrote back that I had great potential... AFTER I took their multi-dollar training course. We really couldn't afford it, but somehow, Mom managed.

Fortunately, I had no aspirations of becoming a star, but it was kind of fun and I got to be in a few "gang" scenes for probably unheard of movies and pose for Ray Vogue Photography School for a free portfolio. That contact came in handy a couple of years later when I fell, literally, for **Jack Palance**.

As a sophomore in high school, I was still a social blah, but I wanted to be on the school paper... the Calumet Crier. So I signed up for Mrs. Hultenschmidt's journalism class. She gave me the confidence to write articles which I slipped into the newspaper office when no one was there. Eventually, I got caught and was made co-editor of the second page with **Dick Trentlage**, an amazing young man who played guitar and had his own band -- The Trent Trio with his brother Bill --and a cute girl singer, Dee Wood. She sang Sioux City Sue like nobody else before or after and always dressed the part with pinafore and pigtails.

Trentlage made everything fun. He sort of took me under his wing and made me feel like I belonged. Always a bit different – if not strange in a nice sort of way – he created his own "trolley car" from a 1930 Model A Ford. As he recalls, "It had French glass doorknobs, a bell clanger in the back seat floorboard, screaming yellow faux-straw woven seats (from the early Red Rocket Chicago streetcars), 'Read as You

Ride' wall dispensers which he used for road maps, an air-powered Wolf Whistle to salute the ladies (young and old) and an old fashion *AAA-OOO-GA* claxon horn."

Highly efficient, the front seat back-rest could be unhooked and swiveled upward to make a picnic table requiring the front seat passengers to re-seat themselves facing the back seat riders. Very handy for picnics in the rain. And an early sign of Trentlage's exceptional creative genius.

I remember riding in the *Trentlage Trolley Car* to a journalism class picnic where one of the sophomores showed off the Piper Cub he was learning to fly. Exercising my reporter daredevil instinct, I coaxed him into letting me fly with him, even though he wasn't licensed for passengers. He agreed, and the minute we hit the air, my old friend motion sickness kicked in. I threw up all over the plane. We landed safely but the rest of that day was no picnic for me. I spent it cleaning up the plane.

Years later, 1962, I visited Dick Trentlage at his home in Fox River Grove, Illinois outside of Chicago. He had just finished writing the *"I wish I were an Oscar Mayer Wiener"* jingle which he recorded in his basement studio with his nine and ten year old children. He had always been involved with music as a member of ASCAP and had been writing rhymes (poetry) since he was eight years old which was the backbone of his future jingle writing.

"Linda (his daughter) had a stuffy nose at the time of recording," he recalls, "But we recorded anyway which was a good thing because Oscar Mayer, himself, commented that every mother had a kid with a cold."

More than fifty years later, Linda, who is now a Director of Curriculum for the Wisconsin Dells school District, is still introduced as the *Oscar Mayer Weiner kid*.

At the time he created the infamous jingle, Trentlage was working for a competing ad agency, but slipped the jingle onto the proper desk at the J. Walter Thompson agency at the crack of dawn on deadline day...and waited.

More than a year later, he was notified that his jingle had won the competition out of 203 entries. The rest is history. Royalties paid for his kids' college education while they were still in elementary school and he is still collecting because it is still running, fifty-six years later. Only the Chiquita Banana jingle has run longer and is listed in the Guinness Book of Records. But that could change since the Chiquita jingle has been altered, and by 2019, the Weiner might replace the Banana. That is Trentlage's fondest dream.

What surprised Trentlage most was that the jingle was requested by radio listeners just like a hit song and symphony orchestras played it at concerts.

And, he didn't stop there. A prominent long time member of ASCAP, Dick partnered in his own jingle-writing business ADVER/SONIC Productions while a writer/producer/music man for McCann Erickson, an international ad agency. His many successes include: TUMS for the tummy, T-U-M-S; Swing to the real thing...Coca Cola; Buckle Up for safety Buckle Up!; Montgomery Wards; McDonald's is your kind of place", and the ever-popular..."WOW! It sure doesn't taste like tomato juice! (V-8). Overall, Trentlage estimates he has written 100 to 250 jingles, but nothing to match his ode to the wiener.

To learn more about Richard Trentlage, his many jingle successes and how to become a jingle writer yourself, read his book, *What's the Big Idea? How to create mind-sticking Ad Jingles that move the goods!*

Destined for stardom in her own right, **Dee Wood** went on to become a backup singer and dancer on many popular television shows in the 50's and 60's including the Pat Boone Show. She is now on the adjunct faculty for speech communications at College of the Desert in Palm Desert, California and "starring" in movements to save and improve conditions for community college faculties nationwide.

When the call came at Calumet High for an editorial representative for the Downtown Shopping News teen section, a Junior Achievement project, I volunteered. The city-wide free-delivery paper reached over four million readers each week. Our job was to organize high school newspaper editors across the city into an elite group who were invited to interview stars as they appeared in stage revues at Chicago's downtown elegant movie houses... the Oriental, the Chicago and the State & Lake. We also wrote a page, *Hy Shopper*, in the newspaper.

By having the articles appear in hundreds of area school papers, parents and students were encouraged to shop downtown and the *stars* got to promote their movies by reaching millions of students and their families.

Another Hi Shopper advantage was getting to know the executive board of Junior Achievement, a high powered group of Chicago's leading businessmen volunteers who guided the fledgling companies. Then advertising tycoon, Hayes MacFarland, owner of MacFarland Aveyard Advertising Agency on North Michigan Avenue, took me under his wing. He introduced me to the steering committee for the development of the still famed *North Michigan Avenue Magic Mile* which included upgrading and revamping buildings with the Water Tower as the focal point. I got to sit in on meetings and offer ideas. I was full of them!

MacFarland also offered me the opportunity to have my own radio show to promote Junior Achievement companies on WOAK-FM in Oak Park on the north side of Chicago. The assignment required me to interview outstanding J. A. teenage entrepreneur executives who ran their Junior Achievement companies and interview them on air. Junior Achievement is an international effort to acquaint young people with initiating businesses, selecting a product category, producing whatever product decided upon and control company operations from producing the product to keeping accounting records to marketing and selling it.

Scheduled to air weekly, the show had to be scripted. I knew nothing about script writing, but learned that the Northwestern School of Journalism offered script writing courses at its downtown Chicago branch. Since I was only sixteen at the time and was still in high school, I had to get special permission to take the course which was taught by a radio station WGN scriptwriter. I loved the class and somehow managed to keep up with the older students.

Later, when writing copy for radio and television, I always remembered the teacher's warning: "look for double meaning phrases when writing copy because you can be sure someone will catch it and the the station will be in jeopardy". His example: an announcer was interviewing a sailor live on air. The sailor explained that his men always landed on the beach first...in waves. "And how many sailors does it take to make a wave?" The station manager went crazy. WAVES were the female part of the Navy.

I finished the course and turned out some pretty good scripts. We probably did twenty shows or more. It was a great experience for me and really paid off as I got involved with radio and television commercial writing later on.

I know times have changed when practically no one recognizes the *big name stars* I interviewed back in 1944-5 who, for the most part, have gone to that big theater in the sky and the current generation doesn't have a clue to who they are.

The Chicago, Oriental and State-Lake were the jewels in downtown Chicago's movie theater crown. They all showed first rate films and had some of Hollywood's best performers on stage between movie showings. The Chicago was the epitome of elegance and grandeur. It was a dream come true for me to meet the stars at this amazing place.

Opened in 1921, the Chicago was –and still is – an elaborately decorated theater with marble columns, dazzling crystal chandeliers and red-carpeted stairways. In its heyday, the Chicago attracted many of the city's well-to-do citizens, mainly women, who could safely enjoy a movie and a great show, most often a popular all-white jazz band performance. Unfortunately, there was a strong color stigma in Chicago in the early twenties and ladies of means did not patronize the predominantly black jazz clubs on Chicago's South Side which featured such greats as Louis Armstrong and Fats Waller. They were missing a lot!

Designed by theater architects C.W. And George Rapp, the 5000 seat Chicago was patterned after elaborate seventeenth century European palaces setting a tone of aristocracy and wealth. It was the prototype for other, less elaborate movie houses, which opened throughout the city. I think the Southtown, located in my part of South Chicago, was one of them.

The Chicago Theater closed in 1985, but public and private efforts enabled it to reopen as a concert venue a year later with an opening performance by Frank Sinatra followed by Aretha Franklin, Johnny Mathis, Al Jarreau, Patti LaBelle, Barry White and many others.

Shortly after the Chicago Theater opened in 1926, the Oriental Theater, also designed by the Rapp Brothers, was deemed to be an Oriental palace, a virtual Asian art museum, with turbaned ushers, Indian-influenced figures, giant Buddhas and the "hashish-dream decorated" auditorium where some of the Hy-Shopper star interviews were conducted.

Judy Garland, Al Jolson, Fanny Brice, Alice Faye, The Three Stooges, George Burns & Gracie Allen, Sophie Tucker and Duke Ellington were just a few notables featured on stage.

In the 1970s, the Oriental changed management many times and abandoned movies for live stage appearances of headliners including Stevie Wonder, Gladys Knight and the Pips and Little Richard.

Still badly in need of repair, the Oriental Theatre was added to the Federal National Registry of Historic Places which saved it from the wrecking ball. In1996, Chicago Mayor Richard Daley announced that the Oriental would be restored to its original grandeur for the presentation of live stage musicals. *Ragtime* opened the revived theater in 1999. It was later that it was renamed the Ford Center for the Performing Arts.

Both the Oriental and the Chicago theaters are a part of the city's downtown history and today's theater promotion – Broadway in Chicago.

I became a regular backstage Janey at both theaters. Lou Breeze, the house orchestra leader at the Chicago, became a really good friend and I always stopped by to chat with him. I was also lucky that a south side neighbor of mine, George Lucas worked there, giving me the opportunity to get backstage even if a Junior Achievement interview was not scheduled. He co-owned the Auburn Park Lucas & Lillian Dance Studio on the south side.

Janis Page was my first official Hi Shopper interview. There was always a photographer on hand, either a high school student or a professional, so I sometimes got to pose with stars and she was one of them. I used the photos with my article which usually appeared in the Cal Crier and/or the Auburn Parker.

To a teen aged girl, Paige was a sophisticated, very friendly and natural person who, as my article noted, "loved gumdrops". She was discovered at the Hollywood Canteen singing *One Fine Day* for the servicemen who chose her name, Janis, from World War I entertainer Elsie Janis. Paige was her grandmother's name. Coincidentally, her first movie was *Hollywood Canteen.* As of 2005, she was still alive, though not performing.

Billy DeWolfe was another one of my first interviews. He was one of those gone but hopefully not forgotten comedians who was considered prime time in the late 40s through 50s. At the Hi-Shopper gathering backstage at the Chicago, the excitement was electric as young and old clamored for a glimpse of the mustachioed jokester with the twinkling eyes and a coveted autograph to give away.

We were the lucky ones; smugly gathered in his dressing room while other stars on the bill, like popular singer-of-the-times Georgia Gibbs, dashed back and forth before "going on". I remember Georgia being a little confused as to where her spot was on-stage, so a stage hand helpfully shoved her forward and another stopped her at the mike. A good catch. But back to Billy. A member of the Jones family of Boston, he dreamed of stardom from the very beginning...as an usher "I was quite a show-off, and so it was only natural that I should be laying people in the aisles," he quipped, or at least that's what my July 1, 1948 article said. His first stage appearance was actually an accident.

One of the acts scheduled to appear at his theater didn't show up, so Billy's boss put him on stage as a replacement since he could sing and dance and, mostly, clown. The audience loved him and it was the start of a longtime career. His boss's name was *DeWolfe* so, in his honor, Billy Jones became Billy DeWolfe and a hit on stage, on broadway, in movies and on television.

Most popular of his skits was *Mrs. Murgatroid*, a plumpish middle age lady with a flowery hat doing lunch alone and bemoaning her fate as an unappreciated housewife, guzzling martini after martini until she was quite inebriated. The skit was an instant hit, repeated in the movie *Blue Skys* and on countless television sit coms and talk shows. DeWolfe was a regular on the Johnny Carson show and brought down the house with his lisping answer to "What have you been doing lately?"... "Busy... buzzy... bizzzzzzzzy!"

He was also a regular on *That Girl* as Mr. Jarvis, Marlo Thomas' acting coach; *Good Morning World,* and *The Queen and I.* He made nineteen movies, most notably *Lullaby of Broadway* and *Tea for Two* with his good friend Doris Day who he nicknamed Mrs. Bixby.. "because she just looked like a Mrs. Bixby." he claimed. DeWolfe was the voice of *Frosty the Snowman*. He died of cancer in 1974 at age 67.

Don DeFore was the glamor boy of the day. A native of Cedar Rapids, Iowa, he always knew he wanted to act and gave himself a self-start by writing plays that only he could star in. Side tracked by a few months at Iowa State University in pre-law, the soft spoken DeFore headed for the Pasadena Playhouse where he studied with classmates Robert Cummings, Victor Mature and Dana Andrews.

Warner Bros. put him under contract where he made a few movies, starred in a few Broadway plays and returned to the screen in *It Happened on Fifth Avenue*, the *Affairs of Susan*, *Ramrod, Thirty Seconds Over Tokyo* with Van Johnson and many others, including his favorite--*You Came Along* which boasted many adlibbed scenes, taking him back to his playwriting days as a child.

DeFore's ambition was to do Shakespeare and he regretted that he was typecast as a broad-comedy player rather than a serious actor.

Our paths crossed a couple of years later when he was shooting a movie in Chicago with some scenes on the front steps of my Phi Gamma Nu Sorority House on Division and Rush streets on the near north side of the city where I lived while attending Northwestern School of Journalism. The one thing I noticed then – he was rather short. When they shot the scenes, he had to stand a step or two above his leading lady to make them "even".

Television discovered DeFore (born DeForest) in the 1950s. He played Thorny Thornberry on the *Ozzie & Harriet Show*, George Baxter with Shirley Booth on the *Hazel Show* and guested on many shows including

Alfred Hitchcock Presents, My Three Sons, Murder She Wrote and *St. Elsewhere*. He died of a heart attack in 1993 at the age of 80.

Born David Daniel Kaminsky in 1913 in the Brownsville area of Brooklyn, New York, **Danny Kaye** literally bubbled over with energy, charming his Hy Shopper audience with his infectious grin and wild gestures.

Danny Kaye was a show stopper even at the press conference. He and his wife, comedy writer Sylvia Fine, had just welcomed daughter Dena, their first and only child, when we interviewed him. Our group presented him with a pair of baby shoes which he promptly put up to his nose (which he refused to alter to please studio heads) and clowned..."They just fit!"

A high school dropout at 13, Danny ran away to Florida and became a street singer. Later, he traveled to the Catskills *Borscht Belt* (Jewish vacation resorts) performing as a comedian and later joining the dance team of Dave Harvy and Kathleen Young. He actually learned to sing and dance and put it all together while in the Orient, the source of his famous "scat" routine and first professional performances.

Continuing our conversation after the official press conference, Danny posed for a picture with me and invited me to have dinner with him after his next show. Breathlessly, I accepted and went out into the audience to watch his show just one more time. He was absolute dynamite, displaying all of the talents I had read about – singing, dancing, double talking. He named 54 Russian composers in 38 seconds in his famous *"Tchaikovsky"* song and often threw in stray Japanese phrases in other "scats". He conducted the Lou Breeze orchestra which he kept on its toes by constantly changing tunes, tempo and sound level.

He was jumping and cavorting wildly across the stage, many times coming dangerously close to the edge which he finally missed and landed in the orchestra pit, breaking his leg...and our dinner date. He repeated the calamity during a performance in *Two by Two,* his own Broadway musical during which he fell and hurt his hip, but he continued to perform for ten minutes to finish the show.

An irreplaceable humanitarian, Kaye was so identified with UNICEF that he was selected to accept the Nobel Prize for them in 1965. He performed for servicemen overseas and for royalty in England, the only time the

Queen requested seating in one of the front rows of the theater rather than in the royal box.

As a conductor, Eugene Ormany invited him to take up the baton to lead his famous orchestra, even though Kaye claimed he couldn't read a note of music. He added fun and spontaneity to the task, one time conducting "Flight of the Bumble Bee" with a fly swatter and keeping time by lying down and kicking his feet. His *Live from Lincoln Center: An Evening with Danny Kaye* broadcast was partially responsible for his 1981 Peabody Award.

Always the clown in such pictures as *Secret Life of Walter Middie, White Christmas*, and many other musical comedies on Broadway. Kaye won an Emmy award for his first season of *The Danny Kaye Show*. In1981, Kaye at last got to show his acting versatility in his final TV film, *Skokie,* for which he received rave reviews for his portrayal of a Nazi concentration camp survivor.

Kaye was a UNICEF ambassador and made the world a better place wherever he went. Danny Kaye died of a heart attack in Los Angeles, California on March 3, 1987. He was 74. It was noted in his memorial that he always wanted to be a doctor... and he was. A doctor of laughter, and there is no better medicine. There will never be another Danny Kaye.

Tony Martin was debonair and oozing with charm. We met him backstage and fired our, what we thought, AP-quality (Associated Press) questions and he responded politely.

Born Alvin Morris on Christmas Day in 1913, in Oakland, California, he received a soprano saxophone from his grandmother and was an instrumentalist and boy soprano while in high school where he formed his first band, *The Red Peppers.* In the 30s, he moved to Hollywood and became *Tony Martin*. He was married to singer/actress Alice Faye from 1936 to 1941 and they starred together with Shirley Temple in *The Poor Little Rich Girl,* the first of his 31 movies ending with a cameo appearance in *Dear Wonderful in 1982.*

In 1948, he married leggy ballet dancer Cyd Charisse which has lasted more than half a century. He still (2007) makes occasional singing appearances for charity. Charisse passed away in June, 2008.

Debbie Reynolds and **Carlton Carpenter, Jr.** who were about the same age as I (sixteen) at the time were great interviews and much fun. They were appearing at the Oriental Theatre to promote one of their first movies *Two Weeks with Love* with Jane Powell, Louis Calhern and Ricardo Montalban. *Abba Dabba Honeymoon* and *Three Little Words* which they sang in the picture were their stepping stones to future fame.

When I arrived, they had just finished their stage act and were running to the back of the theater talking and giggling like any other teenagers. I introduced myself and we had a great chat. They explained that they had never gotten a chance to see the whole movie and were taking the opportunity of sitting back and enjoying it at the Oriental. And so did I.

By my senior year, Hy-Shopper was fading and the group eventually disappeared as did the Downtown Shopping News. I spent my summer vacation between high school and college as *The Soldier's Friend.* Actually, I was the assistant to ex-WAC officer Blanche Osborn who wrote the daily *Soldier's Friend* column for the Chicago Herald American, one of Hearst's newspapers no longer in print.

She was a salty old lady who brought her dalmatian to work every day. My job was to sift thought the many letters she received from GIs and pick a few that she could use in her column. Sometimes I even got to write the column. Most of the time, I greeted veterans who came up to the office to ask specific questions about their entitlement, health issues as related to the service, financial advice and just all kinds of topics. It was a fun job but I had to leave to start college.

Rita Zenzen,
Auburn Parker. First
writing job.

Me & Danny Kaye

Mel Torme, my first
interview.

Autographed by Don
DeFore

Best Wishes from Billy DeWolfe

Rita Zenzen, ace flyer/reporter.

Interviewing at the Chicago Theater. Not a lot of changes from its 1930 opening.

Classmate Dick Trentlage. He wrote, "I wish I were an Oscar Mayer Wiener..." and many more jingles.

Rita Zenzen and classmate Shirley McMillan with Janis Paige.

Debbie Reynolds and Carlton Carpenter, Jr. My last Hy-Shoppe interview

Autographed by Tony Martin

Me and Junior Achievers on WOAK-FM.

Oriental/Ford Center

CHAPTER 2

Stars Plus Strippers

After two years as NOT the million dollar baby in a five and ten cent store, I wanted to do something more exciting and lucrative. Neighbor lounge pianist Norm "Hots" Michaels suggested that I interview with his booking agents, Felix Medlevine and Bob Price, newcomers to the entertainment booking business.

Meeting Felix Medlevine and Bob Price for the first time in their newly furnished quarters off South State Street in downtown Chicago, I now see them as a 1940s version of *The Producers.* After talking with me a few minutes, they excused themselves to go behind the closed doors of Medlevine's office. As they argued back and forth, thinking I couldn't hear them through the paper-thin walls, they came out and agreed that I should be hired. I would take the late shift, 5 to 9 pm. Myrna Torme, Mel's sister, was the daytime receptionist.

My duties, the usual telephone answering, light typing and coffee making PLUS contact acts for clients, work up contracts and keep the bosses from killing each other. Two completely different types, Medlevine owned a clothing store on Maxwell Street and was a typical Jewish merchant with absolutely NO contact with the showbiz world, which meant he had to rely on Price, a real hustler in the brash carnival style of Colonel Tom Parker, Elvis Presley's long-time manager.

Price would turn in false expense accounts, cheat on acts' commissions and, overall, Medlevine's hard earned cash to his own advantage. Each evening they would have an argument about something, being very civil to each other until they slammed the door and the shouting match began. Once they were argued out, they would come out all smiles, thinking that no one had heard a word they said. It was a joke!

They didn't have many acts to book, but always claimed that what they did have was the best. Like the lady comedian we sent out of town who was sent back within hours. She was too risque for the lounge they booked her in. Myrna and I would laugh as we changed shifts and she would relate what happened during the day and what to look out for in the evening. She also kept me up to date on her brother, Mel, who was heading for his second marriage (there were five in all) which she said he was sure would last because he designed a ring with a cross and the star of David which should magically close any religious gaps and put their union in God's hands.

After just a few months of constant combat between Medlevine and Price, I arrived one afternoon to a totally vacant office. Price had cleaned Medlevine out of everything. And Myrna and I were out of a job.

Once again, my neighbor "Hots" Michaels came to the rescue. He referred me to his new agent, **Al Dvorin.**

My first encounter with Al Dvorin, a giant of a man with curly black hair a thick mustache and easy going manner, was scary to say the least. But his big warm smile and twinkly eyes put me at ease in no time. Located on the sixth floor of the Woods Theater Building off State & Monroe in downtown Chicago (since demolished) the Al Dvorin Agency consisted of two private offices and a large reception area with a couple of desks. Unlike, Medlevine and Price, this was a happy, congenial place. **Tommy Diskin**, who ultimately became Colonel Tom Parker's right hand man and Elvis Presley's business manager, was an instant ally and we had great fun together.

Diskin was attending Loyola University in downtown Chicago studying business while working for the Dvorin

Agency which helped him in his future career with the Colonel and Elvis. He was a small very quiet guy with a good sense of humor and a big heart. We were both on a very tight budget, but one day, he invited me out to dinner and a movie. Dinner was at the White Castle (nickel hamburgers) around the corner from the office and the movie was a disaster. We walked around looking at marquees and finally settled on one nearby that he could afford. Imagine our shock when we entered and they were selling sex items in the aisle. The movie was actually a documentary on syphilis. Tommy was so embarrassed, apologizing profusely as he blushed. As soon as the lights went out again, we headed for the door.

Big Al occupied one of the two private offices in our suite which had a fire escape at the back. Paul Frumpkin, an independent agent, occupied the other. The rest of the space was very versatile. When booking income was down, we rented the extra desk space by the hour. And when things were really slow, Al would bring in various and sundry items to sell over the counter in the middle of the reception area.

This is also where I encountered my first stripper...in the file drawer, of course. Strippers were popular everywhere, but Al had exceptional booking contacts in Cicero and other "ganglands" surrounding Chicago. Remnants of the Al Capone gang were still quite obvious on the club scene, especially in small gang-run cities.

One day, a stripper "rush order" came in from one of these locales. All of our regulars were booked, so Al suggested I go through the files and find ANYTHING. And, anything I found. It was a yellowed photo of a shapely lady that looked like something out of the early twenties. Turned out that was exactly where she had come from.

"Write up the contract and have her pick it up here on her way out," Al ordered. When she arrived, I realized she must have been out of the stripping business for quite some time, at least thirty years. But we sent her on her way.

"Let's see," Al pondered, looking at his watch, "it should take her an hour or so to get there. We'll get a phone call, and she'll probably be back here before the day is over. We can tell them that at least we tried." he grinned. And, sure enough, she came back as Al had predicted.

Another "short termer" was a gig for a VFW group that wanted a few exotic dancers for a party. After assuring Al that it was a strictly private affair and absolutely no tickets would be sold, they paid him up front. He agreed to send a few girls for a 30-minute show. But, just to be sure, we drove them to the location and found the guys selling tickets on the street corner. What to do?

Al explained to the ladies that they would go in, do a little dance (with clothes on) and leave quickly...very quickly! We were waiting for them outside and sped away with the party patrons shouting and shaking fists. Next morning, as we expected, the group returned to the office and demanded their money back. A born diplomat, Al convinced them that they had gotten a good deal. No interference from the law, and they should be happy...unless they would like to be reported. They left, but probably not happy!

The secret to successful stripping in those days was, as they said in *Gypsy, (*the story of Gypsy Rose Lee), *Ya Gotta Have A Gimmick.* Her gimmick was the sophisticated tease strip. Our stable of stripper pros took milk baths, carried fans (Sally Rand), had themed costumes (cowboys, Indians). Whatever it took to stand out. One of our most steady booking spots was the Rialto in downtown Chicago. According to today's standards, these strippers were saints. They were required by law to wear pasties over their breast nipples and g-strings over their most private part. Today, they let it all hang out.

One thing I learned about strippers was that they were not really shady ladies. Most of them had a husband and children and needed a job that paid well and allowed them to spend their daytime hours at home with their children, while their daytime working husbands took over in the evening. The real pros looked at stripping as an art. It was a refreshing revelation.

Female impersonators were another type of entertainer that I did not know about. They, too, were popular at little clubs outside of Chicago. And, the performers and their friends were among Al's best customers for the steak knives, artificial corsages and other junk "you can't live without" that he sold from his over-the counter showroom.

Al Dvorin got bitten by the entertainment bug while in the Army overseeing officers' and enlisted men's clubs overseas, providing beverages and entertainment.

Once released, he followed up his contacts and went into booking and entertainer management.

Esther and her Accordion, Betty Chappel and **Jerri Southern**, who appeared on one of the first live TV shows on WBKB-TV, Chicago's first television station were among his *stars.* Southern later made a few records and became mildly successful, although we thought Chappel was the most talented.

Local talent also included the Ross Martin Trio, featuring the popular piano-bass-drum combination. Many of the clubs were still "influenced" by the Al Capone mob, but no one ever acknowledged it. Some of the acts we sent on the road included the Three Little Dickens (actually three of Tommy Diskin's sisters) and a black quartet who we booked all over the country in popular clubs in the "white" sections of the city. But they could never find accommodations in "that part of town". They were forced to retreat to the rundown black areas. It was not a good situation. Until then, I had not realized the scope of segregation in America. It was the late 40's and it seemed that the Civil War may have freed the slaves, as such, but after all that time, life for the blacks did not get much better.

Because I needed extra cash, Al managed to convince some of the major booking agencies in Chicago like MCA, Mutual and McConky to use me to write "press manuals" for some of their acts. I got paid about $25 per manual (terrific for the times) and got a lot of experience writing show biz promotional copy which was valuable in my later advertising/public relations career.

I wrote the commercials for our WBKB-TV show which ran live late in the evening. It was a real challenge writing copy, applying my WOAK-FM radio experience, for the practically illiterate owners of small companies who wanted to demonstrate their product and talk about it themselves for an ego trip. It was my first experience writing and producing TV commercials and the basis for many future ventures.

One of the most unusual shows Dvorin produced was for the deaf. We had a few of our acts in it, but the headliner was **Jimmy Durante**. He was a doll. He could tell I didn't have much backstage experience and tried to put me at ease. We had to laugh and wonder how the show was being appreciated by those who couldn't hear. I have never forgotten him.

Always creative, Al got his staff of two together (Tommy Diskin and me) to brainstorm on finding a new act to offer clients. After tossing ideas back and forth, we came up with a plan to "create a comedian". Al reasoned that he could pick up anyone off the street and turn him into a comic. And that's how Rusty Fields came to be.

Al found him somewhere on skid row, an alcoholic with some obvious comedic talent, cleaned him up and worked with him while Tommy and I began the promotion campaign: calling clubs around Chicago asking them when Rusty Fields was going to appear at their establishment.

Naturally, they never heard of him. But after a few more calls to check on his appearance, club managers got interested and began calling booking agents around town to find out who and where Rusty Fields was. When they finally got to the Al Dvorin Agency, they found Rusty Fields... and Al found a new star. Rusty only lasted a short time because, eventually, the bottle got the best of him. Again. But he was a star for a while.

Another method of finding new talent, and making a little extra cash for the agency, was "Star Audition Night" at small clubs and lounges around the city....some sleazy in sleazier locations. Al would place a classified ad announcing auditions at such and such address (not mentioning that it was a lounge) and young talent responded like crazy. Some good like the Sarah Vaughn and Frank Sinatra almost-sound-alikes; some awful like the young girl acrobat who performed on a bar with inebriated patrons cheering her on.

But the gig gave them all experience and a few went on to bigger and better things. As a matter of fact, some of them became auditioning night regulars and attracted attention from other booking agents in the area who became aware of Al Dvorin's unusual auditions and sometimes attended.

Paul Frumpkin, a bespectacled mild mannered man who specialized in placing exotic dancers (strippers), occupied the second "private" office in the Dvorin agency where he auditioned stripper hopefuls on the "casting couch"... door closed, of course.

One of his rules was: "Never open my office when I am not here!"

Naturally, we abided by his rule...until after he left. Because he had a window in his office which helped cool the place down, we would open it and the door to take advantage of the cross breeze. One day, however, a big wind blew in and slammed the door shut, shattering the frosted glass into a million pieces.

Al calmly got a broom, swept up the pieces, closed the door and locked it. Next morning, Paul came in, said "Good Morning", unlocked his door and began work at his desk. Not until Al stepped through the door did he realize what had happened. Paul was livid, but he got over it in a few days. Nobody could resist Al's big happy grin and attitude for long.

Keeping in touch with acts out of town was always an ongoing challenge with the phone company. Al would have the acts call collect and ask for a non-existent person. Then he would manage to discreetly exchange information, refuse to accept the charges and hang up. After a while, Ma Bell got wise and a supervisor called to warn him that they knew what he was doing and it had to stop. He casually told the operator to "go play with yourself". The agency's phone service was suspended for a day or two.

One of the much lesser-known stars we booked was Denna, a big busted dumb brunette who could not sing, but could attract male companionship. In those days, non-talented females became "B" girls. They would sing off key and then get customers to buy them drinks (water with a slice of lemon) and get a percentage off of the profits from the club.

Denna had a tremendous crush on Al and fancied herself his girlfriend. She would drop in practically daily wearing a slouched hat (we could hear her clomping down the hallway) and Al would immediately close his door and head for the fire escape where he stayed until she left which was often a very long time. Denna always wanted to give us a report on her success at a lounge she had been booked at and one day stunned us with... "The nicest thing happened to me last night. One of the customers said I was a slut. That is good, isn't it?" What could we say?

Direct mail was a big thing with Al. I was always creating post cards and fliers promoting our stable of talent, addressing them and stuffing big boxes to be mailed... some day. A few years later, when I stopped in Chicago to visit, the agency was not in its old place. It had moved from the sixth to the eighth floor. When I finally found it, Al explained that so many boxes of mail had stacked up in the old office that there wasn't enough room to work. So he locked the doors and moved upstairs to start over.

Al and I exchanged Christmas cards through the years. He married Bernice and they had three children, Shirley, Rabbi James Dvorin and Wendy. Al Dvorin become a star in his own right. Through Tommy Diskin, Al met Colonel Tom Parker. They immediately hit it off and from then on, Al devoted all of his time to booking Elvis Presley concerts and emceeing his shows. At one of these, the Colonel informed Al that Elvis would not be doing an encore which prompted his off-the cuff remark, *Ladies and Gentlemen...Elvis has left the building.*

Dvorin was nicknamed *Sweet Al* by the Elvis entourage because of his sweet disposition, "not because of my sexual orientation" he would laugh. He appeared in a couple of Elvis movies and spent twenty-two years working with Elvis and Colonel Parker, longer than any other Elvis employee

After Elvis' death, Al was invited to join a group of Elvis impersonators and devotees who put together shows remembering Elvis. Al Dvorin became an important part of the team and performed in many concerts relating his Elvis memories in his inimitable amusing voice including the renowned "Aloha from Killarney" concert featuring the Emerald Elvis.

On August 22, 2004, on his way from Palm Springs to a Remember Elvis concert in Las Vegas with Ed Bonja, Tom Diskin's nephew, Al Dvorin was tragically killed when the car he was a passenger in (Bonjo driving) swerved past a curve and down an enbankment. It happened less than a year after his beloved wife Bernice succumbed to cancer and he was just getting back into the swing of his Remember Elvis gigs. Dvorin had collected an enormous amount of Elvis' artifacts from his 1955 to 1977 tenure and had always planned to put his memories of Elvis in a book, but never got to it. Al was never very organized and was not computer friendly enough to record his thoughts. I wish I had kept in better contact and maybe could have helped him make his wish come true.

The last Christmas card I got from Al Dvorin and Bernice, was in 2003 with a photo of Al on the cover with his famous quote...*Elvis has left the building.* Only this time, it was "sweet" Al Dvorin who had left. He is a show biz icon who deserves to be remembered. I know I'll never forget him. He had a great influence on my future and I still think of him.

After graduating from Calumet high school, I enrolled at the University of Illinois-Navy Pier Branch, originally a Naval training station and now a giant entertainment complex. Bored with classes and needing to earn more money than a part time job could offer, I decided to return to Northwestern School of Journalism's downtown Chicago campus as a part-time student. I moved into the Phi Gamma Nu sorority house at 25 East Division Street (now a bed and breakfast) and reduced my star citing to visiting with jazz great **Muggsy Spanier** at the Blue Note and a wannabe opera singer at a Rush Street pizza parlor. Spanier opened at the Blue Note, a cellar club on Madison and Dearborn, in 1947 and played there off and on until 1955. He got to know me from my coming in and waived the club's cover charge for me.

I had to take some non-star type jobs like writing info-sign copy for Sears and editing text books on *How to Service TD-24 Tractors* for International Harvester which had a school off of Maple street on the Gold Coast. The location was great... 936 North Michigan Avenue. The engineers used to stand by the window and watch the ladies get off the bus as the wind blew their skirts over their heads. We officed above Bez Ben crazy custom hat shoppe featuring concoctions of artificial fruits, vegetables and birds atop ridiculous hat shapes priced in the $100+ range. Across the street was the fabulous Drake Hotel where we occasionally saw stars like Tallaluh Bankhead in mink and jeans prancing in and out of the entrance.

One rainy night, I was late for class and I ran into Abbott Hall when my high heels hit a slick spot on the tile floor and I slid right into... **Jack Palance.** He wasn't a movie star then. But he was gorgeous and I couldn't stop blushing and apologizing. He was wonderful, picked me up and asked if I would have dinner with him. I explained that I had to go to class, but could meet him after. Which we did, much to my surprise. I really had no idea he was an actor.

At dinner, I learned that Jack was the understudy to Anthony Quinn in *Street Car Named Desire* which was playing at the Shubert theater in downtown Chicago. (He eventually took over the lead from Marlon Brando on Broadway). He was staying at the Allerton Hotel on North Michigan Avenue. Jack was a true gentleman. He didn't drink, didn't smoke (then) and was very moral. Born Vladimiri Palaniuk, Walter Jack Palance grew up in Pennsylvania, worked in the coal mines and was a professional heavyweight boxer.

He joined the military and received the purple heart, good conduct medal and the World War II Victory Medal before turning to acting in the mid '40s. *Streetcar* was one of his first big breaks and it was really exciting for me and my sorority sisters when he came to pick me up. They would hide in the closet with the door open a crack just to get a glimpse of the gorgeous 6 foot three hunk.

We dated for only a few months...movies, dinner, lunch, breakfast. And I watched the softball games that the Streetcar cast played against the Mr. Robert's cast on Sunday mornings before the matinee. Jack had been dating the understudy to Uta Hagin in Streetcar before coming to Chicago, and finally told me that he would probably marry her. Besides, I was too young for a permanent relationship and he would be leaving Chicago soon.

A couple of years later, he called my home to see how I was doing. My mother was thrilled. But she wasn't so thrilled one night when I had to return to my south side home. He brought me home after midnight and she chewed him out for taking advantage of a young girl. Actually, he was gentleman enough to accompany me on the hour-plus subway-elevated-streetcar ride from downtown Chicago to my far south side home...and back to downtown again! My Mom reprimanded him for bringing me home so late, but later bragged that her daughter dated Jack Palance.

As all fledgling actors, Jack was on a tight budget, but needed a new photo portfolio. So I took him to meet my friends at Ray Vogue School of Photography where I still modeled once in awhile in exchange for photos. He jumped at the chance and they were equally excited to be able to work with a real up-and-coming actor. He gave me one of his earlier photos and wrote a poem on it for me...*a ceiling full of holes, a night full of stars and a little princess, Jack*

Poetry was one of Palance's passions. The other was simulating the fictional character that he was playing or reading about. Free verse was Jack's style and one time, he gave me a few of his works to type. I cheerfully took them home, edited them and brought back the carefully typed verse. He went ballistic! I had rhymed his free verse.

Acting legend Joan Crawford discovered Palance in the early fifties and gave him his first chance in an A picture, *Sudden Fear.* Prior to that, he had appeared in a few B westerns. Watching Sudden Fear, I remembered what Jack had told me about his background. He repeated it in the film as part of the script when he and Crawford were on a train, just talking. He never mentioned, however, that he spoke six languages including Ukrainian (his ancestry): Russian, Italian, Spanish, French and English. He has a star on the Hollywood Walk of Fame, and I read that he had been inducted into the Hall of Great Western Performers of the National Cowboy and Western heritage Museum. Also read that he graduated from Stanford University after he left Chicago with an AB in drama.

I saw Jack twice after that. Once in the 60's while I was poolside at an upscale apartment complex in the toney River Oaks area of Houston. He was still married, but passed by saying "I remember you, but my wife is still jealous". Since then, he remarried. The second time I saw him was accidental, in front of the old Houston Auditorium. He was there to watch a group of Hungarian gypsies perform. I still get a twitch every time I see him on TV or in a movie and am happy to know that his healthy lifestyle, remember the one-armed push-ups he did when accepting the 1991 Best

Supporting Actor Oscar, kept him alive to see his 87th birthday. Jack died in early 2007.

Again out of a job for a few weeks, I was directed to the Bridgeport News in the stockyards/Mayor Richard J. Daley (the first) part of town, which had an urgent need for an editor. I called and they hired me over the phone. Seems their last editor had just called from the bakery where they had sent him to pick up bagels to say he wasn't coming back. After a few weeks there, I could understand why.

I had only one day to put the thirty-some page tabloid together. The front page story was on then alderman John L Daley. I wrote the story and the headline: *Daily Does etc. etc.* Next morning I arrived at the office off south Racine Avenue to find Daley and his bodyguards waiting for me. I had mis-spelled his name and he was really upset. My later dealings with him were at the local movie theater where he was hosting a free movie party for the underprivileged neighborhood children. He stood at the front door, asked the little ones if their parents were going to vote for him and if they answered, "no" or "didn't know", they were turned away. I understand his son, now in office, has a much more humanitarian demeanor.

Sid, Moe and Ellis Feldman owned the Bridgeport News. Three such diverse brothers would be hard to find. Sid was the leader, a hustler and a good businessman. Moe was a whiner and a complainer. Ellis was sweet and considerate and did not seem like a part of the same family.

Each week they would argue and shout about advertising, accounting, circulation...anything to cause disagreement. They did the same thing with advertisers which meant I didn't know how big the paper would be until the last minute on Tuesday afternoon because advertisers would talk first to one brother, and then another, getting conflicting information on price, placement, and just things in general causing cancellation, reinsertion, and back again.

The best thing about the job was Tuesday night when we went to the printer and produced the final paper, winding it up around midnight and stopping for a bowl of matza ball soup before going home.

While at the Bridgeport News, I worked with Jane Addams Hull House, a community settlement project dedicated to helping the poverty-stricken neighborhood and the kids to have a better life with recreational activities, social services, financial aid and helpful advice, especially for the teen agers. For many of the boys, "chicken" was the favorite sport. It involved racing and sideswiping cars. The winner was the one who came out with the least damage.

Still a teenager myself, I invited those interested to form a group which could contribute stories to the Bridgeport News, much the same as Hy-Shopper. They could write a column and I would take them on field trips to gather news. It was heartbreaking to see some of them with real talent for writing or art be discouraged because they didn't think they could rise above their background and surroundings. Most were on welfare with non-nurturing parents.

One of our most memorable field trips was to radio station WIND at the top of the Wrigley Building on Chicago's North Michigan Avenue. **Eddie Hubbard** was the popular disc jockey who had a nightly show and often had celebrity guests. Eddie moved to Chicago from Boston in the mid 1940s and was more than a disc jockey. He hosted shows at Chicago's movie palaces, did live and television broadcasts and eventually wrote some of the scripts for *Hawaiian Eye* and *Love, American Style.*

The night that I took my Hull House kids to the show, we were to interview **June Allyson** and **Dick Powell** who were Hubbard's guests that evening. We took the bus, got to the Wrigly Building on north Michigan Avenue, took the elevator as far as it would go and walked up the last flight of stairs to the top, chatting excitedly as we went. When we opened the door, the waiting crowd shouted, "Here she comes, it's June Allyson!" But it wasn't. It was just me, Rita Zenzen, with a raspy throat giving me the June Allyson sound. Then the real Dick and June arrived. They and Eddie were great, giving "my kids" an interview, autographs and posing for pictures with them.

In 1990, Hubbard moved to Dallas and joined the Satellite Music Network hosting the Stardust oldies show.. Later, he could be heard on KAAM-AM Dallas with his own afternoon show *Hubbard's Cupboard.* I talked to him in the summer of 2006, sent him a copy of his photo with June Allyson and Dick Powell and got his enthusiastic blessing to finish this book. Sadly, like many of my other favorite stars, Eddie Hubbard died on March 26, 2007, of injuries suffered in an automobile accident in Grand Prairie. He was 89.

Another time, I took the group to a TV game show hosted by orchestra leader Frankie Carl. I had been pre-selected as a contestant and we were all excited. I was so excited, in fact, that I flunked the first question... "and what is your name?" I was stunned, I couldn't remember. Needless to say, I didn't win any prize money that trip.

The Bridgeport News is still churning out newspapers every Wednesday and is regarded as one of the best weeklies in Chicago being used as a prototype in Northwestern University's journalism classes. But it has moved from its Racine location to 32nd and Halsted. Hull House is still at 800 S. Halsted. Part of it is a museum and the original as well as a few add-ons are still serving the underprivileged.

A year with the Feldmans was about all I could take, so I went on to greener (moneywise) pastures: editor of *Business Screen* and *See & Hear* magazines. Located just steps away from the Northwestern Chicago downtown campus, the publications were owned by Ott Colin and focused on the then-flourishing 16mm entertainment, training and documentary film industry.

There were no big stars here only popular 16mm producers which would soon be replaced by television gurus. While there, I knew a guy with Philco who was being transferred to Japan. That sounded like a good place to go, so I applied for an information specialist job with the government. My application was accepted and I was packed, ready to go, when I was notified that it was too dangerous for me to move at that time. So, I unpacked and looked for a new job.

I found a new work home just down the street at MacDonald-Cook Advertising Agency, 333 North Michigan Ave. I was hired as public relations assistant to spinster Kansas native, Norma Schuelke. It was a great job. I had interesting accounts and lots of fun things to do. I wrote a syndicated column for Kirsch Drapery Hardware: *Decorating Tips for Your Windows by Kerry Chase* (K.C. **K**irsch **C**ompany, get it); coordinated contests with great trips to Havana, Cuba (in its heyday) for Silvercote Insulation and wrote and produced a bi-monthly magazine for the Trailercoach Dealers National Association which allowed me to seek out stars once again.

Setting up a TV interview for one of our clients brought me to the former Chez Paree, one of Chicago's snazziest night clubs, where **Mike Wallace** and his then-wife Buff Cobb did a talk show. I went over to meet them and set up the deal. I never dreamed that Mike Wallace would go on to become an international news icon. I was getting ready to leave the club when I heard some familiar voices laughing and talking.

Dean Martin and **Jerry Lewis** were the entertainers that week at the Chez and evidently they were getting ready to rehearse and couldn't find Jerry. The group went out the back door and looked around the alley. Pretty soon, there was the familiar ding-a-ling of a bicycling ice cream man. As the sound got closer Martin and his party totally cracked up. Jerry Lewis was riding the bike/ice cream wagon. "Anybody want an ice cream bar?" he cooed.

Putting together a magazine that would appeal to a broad audience and entice readers to become *trailer coach owners* was TDNA's order. So, I went after off-the-wall ideas. While the circus was in town, I worked up a triple whammy involving comedian **Paul Gilbert,** a circus bear, and a family of circus high-fliers who actually traveled from town to town in their trailer coaches.

For the picture, I had Gilbert standing in the doorway of a trailer coach holding the huge circus bear on a leash. The Associated Press photographer was about to shoot the picture when the bear turned toward Paul and growled. Paul screamed, the photographer shot and it was a great picture...but a very nervous Paul Gilbert. At the time, he was married to Barbara Cowan. Melissa (Little House on the Prairie) and Jonathon were their adopted children. After their divorce in1972, Barbara remarried and had daughter Sara, who was a regular on Roseanne. In the mid-50s, I ran into him at the Continental Houston Hotel, (I did their public relations) where he was booked. After fifteen years he still remembered ...the bear!

The family of high fliers, whose name I can't recall, allowed us to photograph their trailercoaches and invited me to join them up on the trapeze platform. I managed to get up to the platform, but when they invited me to fly... I flew... in the other direction. A dare devil I am not.

Ben Blue, who was entertaining at a nearby club, was as somber looking as his trademark. He hardly ever smiled, but that was part of his comic routine, and he was most agreeable to being photographed in a trailer coach wearing his traditional baggy pants and untraditional smile. I managed to get some advance newspaper placement for the shot in addition to the cover of *Living... the Trailer Coach Way*. I was lucky to get him, because shortly thereafter, he concentrated on managing his nightclubs with just a few personal, TV and movie appearances.

The first (and last) summer on the job, boss-Norma's nephew came from Wichita, Kansas to spend the summer with her. I met him, we dated and he invited me to come to Wichita and meet his sister. Since I had never been outside of Chicago, I did and soon returned to learn about living in Wichita. Take it from me, at that time Wichita was NO FUN!

Wichita was small and there was not much work, not much excitement and not much to do. Boeing Airplane Company was the major employer and they did not have anything to offer a hopeful young writer/promoter except an advertising director's job. I applied for it. They thought I was too young and a female, (Wichita was very conservative). But because I was the most qualified they had interviewed, they agreed to consider me.

In order to eat in the meantime, I took a short termer as a dance instructor with Arthur Murray. According to the ad, the job paid $25 a week for training (important: no waiting period for the money).

Three weeks of training included learning to dance the Arthur Murray way, customer relations and how to sell more dance lessons. Then, you were on your own in the studio and your paycheck increased according to how many lessons or renewals you sold.

Watching *So You Think You Can Dance* on television brought back some fond memories, like practicing for a state waltz competition and how to handle students like the little old man who just loved the "jitterbug". With his arm around my waist, it was 1-2-3-rock-.and 1-2-3-rock-and. On the "rock-and" his little old hand slowly traveled up to my breast area which took some diplomatic action on my part; move his hand back to my waist without upsetting him. It evidently worked because he renewed his month's course a couple of times while I was there.

Included in the training was a session on "mood cycles"; tracing a student's mood over a four-week period. It included happy, sad, thoughtful, etc. By keeping a one-month's record, you could predict your students' attitudes and moods every month thereafter. Surprisingly, it really worked and to this day, I find myself charting friends and business associates.

When the call finally came from Boeing, I jumped at the chance of moving on. One of the most fun things I did on that job was write employee recruitment radio commercials. I managed to get them to record the jet takeoff sound of the YB-54 which they were introducing to open the spots. It made the whole commercial and got lots of attention and applicants nationwide.

Overall, Wichita was lonely and boring until one day I got a call from **Tommy Diskin**, my Al Dvorin buddy, who knew I was there. He invited me to meet him and his new employer, **Colonel Tom Parker**, and his client Eddy Arnold at the auditorium to see the show and have something to eat with them later. It was just what I needed.

The show was great. Eddy sang, sold Ralston Purina dog food and after the show rushed to the back of the theater to sell his Eddy Arnold promotional merchandise (string ties and mini covered wagon pins with his name on them), under the direction of Colonel Parker. At the time, I was not aware that the "wagon" was the Colonel's official logo.

After the show, Tommy invited me to join him and the Colonel for a late supper at the local diner. Always the clown, the Colonel ordered Nebo Pie which baffled and flustered the waitress. She nor anyone else had ever heard of Nebo Pie, but eager to please, she asked everybody in the place what Nebo Pie was. No one knew and the Colonel got his kick of the day. Doesn't take much to make some people happy. The next time I saw Tom Diskin and Colonel Parker was at the Shamrock Hotel in Houston, Texas.

One year at Boeing and I headed back to Chicago and my always waiting part time job at the Al Dvorin Theatrical Booking Agency. I wanted to save enough money to go to San Francisco, but at $1.25 an hour, it would have taken a lifetime. So I settled for Houston, Texas.

Al said there were lots of opportunities there. We booked Glenn McCarthy's Shamrock Hotel a few times and things were really humming down there. Al suggested that I call McCarthy, who owned a radio station, a few newspapers, lots of cash-producing oil wells and, of course, the internationally famed Shamrock Hotel, to see where I could fit in. Being naïve and adventurous, I took his advice and boarded the train for Houston, Texas.

Al Dvorin declares "Elvis has left the building!"

Al Dvorin with Elvis impersonator and Tommy Diskin's nephew Ed Bonja

Al Dvorin, Elvis's longest employee

Entertainer Ed Bonja still travelling the Elvis trail.

Sally Rand Al Dvorin didn't have, but some of his strippers seemed left over from her day.

Muggsy Spanier, the man with a horn.

My alma mater, Unversity of Illinois at Navy Pier, now transformed into an entertainment center.

Walter Jack Palance, full of dreams and verse.

B-Westerns groomed Jack Palance for City Slickers.

Eddy Arnold meets Elvis Presley, Colonel Parker's new discovery.

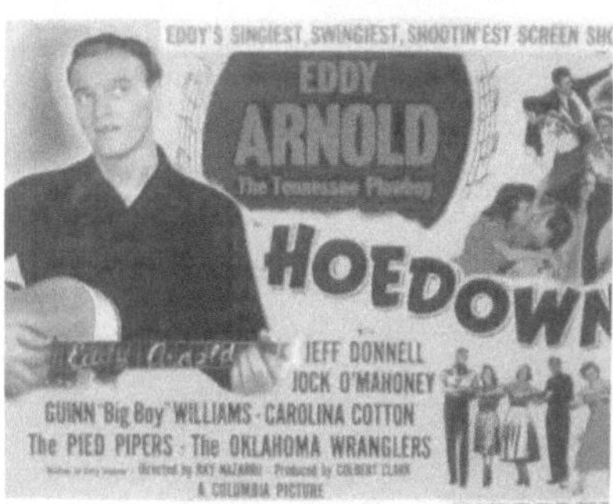

Eddy Arnold, Colonel Parker's first find.

The original Chicago Mayor Daley greets student protesters at U of I at Navy Pier.

Jane Addams Hull House still serves Chicago needy.

June Allyson and Dick Powell greet the Hull House group.

Hull House aspiring teen journalists meet, from left, Eddie Hubbard and sportster Ed McElroy. I'm at the end.

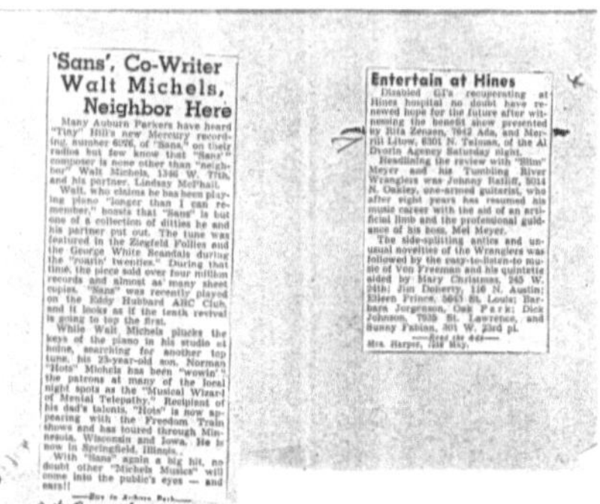

'Sans', Co-Writer Walt Michels, Neighbor Here

Many Auburn Parkers have heard "Tiny" Hill's new Mercury recording, number 6076, of "Sans," on their radios but few know that "Sans'" composer is none other than "neighbor" Walt Michels, 1346 W. 77th, and his partner, Lindsay McPhail.

Walt, who claims he has been playing piano "longer than I can remember," boasts that "Sans" is but one of a collection of ditties he and his partner put out. The tune was featured in the Ziegfeld Follies and the George White Scandals during the "roarin' twenties." During that time, the piece sold over four million records and almost as many sheet copies. "Sans" was recently played on the Eddy Hubbard ABC Club, and it looks as if the tenth revival is going to top the first.

While Walt Michels plucks the keys of the piano in his studio at home, searching for another top tune, his 23-year-old son, Norman "Hots" Michels has been "wowin'" the patrons at many of the local night spots as the "Musical Wizard of Mental Telepathy." Recipient of his dad's talents, "Hots" is now appearing with the Freedom Train shows and has toured through Minnesota, Wisconsin and Iowa. He is now in Springfield, Illinois.

With "Sans" again a big hit, no doubt other "Michels Musics" will come into the public's eyes — and ears!!

Entertain at Hines

Disabled GI's recuperating at Hines hospital no doubt have renewed hope for the future after witnessing the benefit show presented by Rita Zenzen, 7642 Ada, and Merrill Litow, 6301 N. Talman, of the Al Dvorin Agency Saturday night.

Headlining the review with "Slim" Meyer and his Tumbling River Wranglers was Johnny Ratliff, 5014 N. Oakley, one-armed guitarist, who after eight years has resumed his music career with the aid of an artificial limb and the professional guidance of his boss, Mel Meyer.

The side-splitting antics and unusual novelties of the Wranglers was followed by the easy-to-listen-to music of Von Freeman and his quintette aided by Mary Christmas, 245 W. 24th; Jim Doherty, 116 N. Austin; Eileen Prince, 5643 St. Louis; Barbara Jorgenson, Oak Park; Dick Johnson, 7935 St. Lawrence, and Bunny Fabian, 301 W. 23rd pl.

Auburn Parker clips: Norm "Hots" Michaels; Hines Hospital benefit.

Eddie Hubbard was still spinning the oldies across the nation in his 80s.

Eddie Hubbard headlined stage review in addition to his djaying.

CHAPTER 3

Shooting Stars at the Shamrock

After a very long train ride from Chicago, I arrived in Houston,Texas and couldn't believe the weather...and my first palm tree. I thought I was in the tropics. I planned to stay at the downtown YWCA until I could find better quarters and investigate **Glenn McCarthy's** holdings.

I decided I would try his radio station first; KXYZ-ABC. The studios were located downtown, not far from the Y. Also found a classified ad for a roommate to share an apartment with three other girls. In the early fifties, there were not the same dangers as today regarding unkowns sharing.

Actually, the station did not have an opening, but they were thinking about replacing their promotion director. The station manager felt I was perfect for the job. But he had to find a way and time to get rid of the person currently in that slot. In the meantime, I applied to an Arthur Murray Dance Studio to work in their telemarketing program.

A few weeks later, I was notified that the job was mine and I could start the following Monday. Now I had a nice apartment with three new roommates and the beginnings of a great job.

Since there was very little or no television or ipods at the time, radio was a major source of entertainment. KXYZ had a national reputation for being inventive and creative with its programing. It produced and ran live musical shows on a weekly basis and aired Saturday at the Shamrock on the ABC network each Saturday night, the only national show emanating from Texas.

There were also just a few advertising agencies in Houston at the time. A major part of my job was to write and produce commercials, station promos and market Saturday at the Shamrock which featured some of the top stars in the country. Many of them fell in love with the Shamrock and Houston at the hotel's awesome opening and were happy to return as a guest on the show. Kathy Parker was my assistant who we nicknamed "plugger" (she pronounced it "pluuger in a deep southern accent) because she scheduled the show plugs.

Some of the fun commercials I wrote were takeoffs on the popular songs of the day. Example: *How Much Is*

That Doggy in the Window converted to *How Much Is That Used Car in the Window* referring to Dean Warchow Chevrolet's bargain of the day. I don't think anyone ever worried about copyrights then. Maybe we were just lucky.

Fred Nahas was station manager and top personality at KXYZ. Known as the "man with the golden voice", he claimed to be wanted by many stations and even the movies in Hollywood. He was often referred to, in jest, as *Mr. Hollywood.* Fred hosted Saturday at the Shamrock from 1949 until 1953 when the show was canceled. He also did a daily news program, *Tomorrow's History,* which ran weekdays at 6pm. We all helped put it together and I finished the script and handed it to him at the stroke of 6 as he came flying in... just in time to open the show after the first commercial. He was never early.

But most of all, he was Glenn McCarthy's friend and fall guy. Many a night the two would go out on the town and wind up in the middle of a brawl. Next morning, we always knew who didn't win. Fred wound up with a black eye while Glenn had cheered him on from the sidelines. Usually, McCarthy started the fight; Fred had to finish it. One thing about Fred Nahas, he was a happy guy and always open to new ideas from staff members, which he would at first reject and later present them at staff meeting as his own...a few days after they were presented to him.

One of the advantages of working with a leading, innovative radio station was that I could develop and produce programs and commercials and had the talent available to make them happen. Tim Nolan was the cheerful, morning DJ and one of the Saturday at the Shamrock announcers. A pudgy, mustachioed twinkly-eyed Irishman, he had a tremendous following. I tried to write commercials to match the voice and personality of the announcer who was to deliver them and his was the most fun. I still *hear* voices when I write.

Tim's morning show was off-the-cuff and he took chances, playing songs that were a little over the edge, like Johnny Stanley's *It's in the Book*, a rousing takeoff on a gospel tune; and making an occasional naughty slip like, "Ladies, have you checked your panties lately?", which he claimed was a slip of the tongue, he really meant *pantries.*

Nita Renfro, the brash wise-cracking gum-chewing receptionist, kept everybody in stitches and shocked some of the more conservative visitors with her off color comments and jokes. Everyone loved her. The rest of the station personnel were awesome: Jay Froman, a classical singer, hosted Music of the Masters. He was married with a couple of kids. Much later, he starred in Most Happy Fella, at Theatre Under the Stars (a local theater company) in the city's Hermann Park where he met his next wife.

His co-star was Sylvia (can't remember her last name) It was love at first sight followed by marriage (after their respective divorces). Jay is no longer with us. I don't know about Sylvia. I know she continued in musical theater and was the sidekick for Mary Jane Vandivere's daily talk show on Channel 39TV. But that was many, many years ago.

Guy Savage was the brilliant sports director. DJ Larry Naylon and his soulmate, secretary Jackie Powers, wrote the weekly Saturday at the Shamrock scripts under Nahas' direction. Sales manager/ announcer Ken Bagwell, outside promotions man Art Finger and traffic manager Maxine Jones rounded out the regular staff.

Bill Roberts, who did a recap of his daily gossip column running in the long-defunct Houston Press, sat at the desk across from me. At the time he hired a friend, a stay-at-home housewife, as his assistant.

Maxine Messenger later became one of the nation's best known gossip columnists. When the Press folded, Bill made a deal with the Houston Post (also defunct) thinking that Maxine would come along with him. After all, she did most of the legwork and some of the writing. He really needed her. But surprise, surprise! Maxine worked her own deal with the Houston Chronicle and became his biggest competitor.

Bill was fascinated by my maiden name - Zenzen - which he joked was really Neznez spelled backwards. He always reported on my activities in his daily column, like the time my photo-journalism student- teacher assigned me to cover the University of Houston football team.

The instructor said all I had to do was stay on one knee where he put me on the playing field and shoot the team as they came from the lockers. What he didn't say was that they came out running...FAST and waving...not looking... and ran over me. Roberts thought it was hilarious and featured the incident in his column the next day.

Another Bill Roberts remembrance was a séance he and his wife Martha invited us to. It was in a creepy old house on the outskirts of Houston, perfect for spooks.

The group conducting the séance claimed they were going to bring Houdini back. He reputedly would return on Halloween if correctly summoned.

Well, they ran into a lot of difficulties. First, someone came through the front door after the séance started and they all thought it was Houdini, which made me laugh. Then we all held hands and concentrated on Houdini. If he was there, he was supposed to rattle the chandelier. Instead, one of the seancers had a grumbling stomach. The rest of the group turned the lights back on and reprimanded him, claiming his stomach noises scared away Houdini's ghost. Who knows? They planned to try again the next year!

Sometimes Bill had me co-host his weekly *On the Town* radio show which ran after Saturday at the Shamrock, live from the nearby Ding How Chinese restaurant on Main Street. Many times he and I and my then boyfriend were the only ones there. When he declared, "and here we are at the beautiful exciting Ding How restaurant with lots of happy after-theater diners. Let's hear it from you...". And the three of us would scream and clap and stomp and cheer like a full house.

Live music shows that I put together during my tenure at KXYZ included a teen singing/instrumental quartet, the Four Spades: Harry, Larry, Jerry and Joe. The Larry part of the group was 16 year old **Larry Hovis,** who sang I*'m A Long Tall Texan; you oughta see me ride my horse.* My favorote part was the *Gitty up, gitty up, gitty up* which he recited as he bounced as if riding a horse. No wonder he went on to national fame as a singer, comedian and an actor appearing on Gomer Pyle, U.S.M.C., Andy Griffith Show and Hogan's Heros where he played demolition man Sgt. Carter on a regular basis for two years.

Hovis guested on many popular TV shows including Rowen and Martin's Laugh-In. Chico and the Man, Alice, The Doris Day Show and produced several game shows including Liar's Club on which he appeared from 1976 to 1978.

Larry's sister, Joan Hovis, was a nationally known vocalist and helped to get Larry discovered. The other three Spades went on to join popular musical groups in Houston. At the time, I remember Dini Hofheinz,a rather shy bespectacled daughter of oil tycoon and former Houston mayor **Roy Hofheinz,** had a terrific crush on Larry which got the group (and me) invited to a lot of Hofheinz-hosted VIP parties.

Larry Hovis spent his final years as a professor teaching drama at Southwest State University in San Marcos, Texas, He died of cancer in 2003.

In the early 60s, Hofheinz and fellow oil tycoon **R. E. "Bob" Smith** built the nation's first enclosed sports arena – the Astrodome -- with elegant sky boxes for the ultra VIPs like Augie Busch, Bill Marriott, Sr. and so many others. Two more unlike individuals you will never find. Hofheinz was brash and pushy; Smith quiet and laid back. But in business, they seemed to click, like most of the other mismatched partners I knew.

Dick Krueger, a handsome young tenor who sang at the Shamrock's famous Cork Club, had a weekly fifteen minute show on the station and was idolized by the teenagers. He was also the featured vocalist on Saturday at the Shamrock and at the hotel's plush Cork Club. He was once invited to audition on-air for the Don McNeil Breakfast Club, a popular 1940-50's morning variety show on ABC.

They were looking for a replacement vocalist and had heard Dick on Saturday at the Shamrock. What they didn't know was that Dick had a tendency to sing a little off key. Once he started "off" he never got back "on". Shamrock regular orchestra leaders Henry King and Paul Neighbors were aware of the problem and always had the band follow Dick's lead urging him to go up or down as needed instead of the other way around.

Unfortunately, neither orchestra was at the Breakfast Club audition and Dick didn't make the cut. After one airing, they discovered what we all knew, he sometimes sang a little off-key! Krueger didn't get that job, but he continued to be a favorite with Glenn McCarthy and the Shamrock. At least in his '80s, Dick still lives in River Oaks in Houston, still sings and has his own trio to follow his lead at society functions.

Krueger really had a great voice. I was thrilled when he consented to sing at my wedding but he came down with laryngitis the day before. Jay Froman filled in for him. He, too, had a great voice and sang *You'll Never Walk Alone.*

Another show which aired every Saturday morning turned out to be a real winner. **Tommy Sands** was about fifteen when he and his mother came up to the station to see if there might be a spot for him. At the time, I didn't know any of his history. He had come from a musical family, his mother was a vocalist with the Art Castle band in Chicago and his father was a pianist.

An avid country music fan as a child he begged for a guitar, and at age seven, his mother granted his wish. He loved to play and entertain. The family moved to Louisiana where Sands guested on Louisiana Hayride. After his parents' divorce, Tommy and his mother moved to find greener pastures and headed for Houston. Tommy already had radio experience and appeared in many school productions and on radio shows in Louisiana. From my experience with the Dvorin Agency, I recognized that Sands had exceptional talent and agreed to help him if I could. I convinced Fred Nahas that a show with Tommy Sands would be a good attraction for Saturday morning teen audiences. He agreed. So I put something together and we went on air.

At about that time, I got a call from my old Dvorin Agency buddy Tommy Diskin. **Eddy Arnold** was booked into the Shamrock and for a special performance at the Annual Capon Dinner, a charity event started by Bill Williams at his Restaurant on South Main in the 40's with the serving of capon and wild game provided by wealthy hunters who paid a good price to eat and help charitable organizations. The city's leading businessmen have continued the tradition to this day. The restaurant was practically across the street from the Shamrock so it was easy for Eddy to do. And, as in Wichita, he hawked his Eddy Arnold string ties, covered wagon pin and other goodies in back after his performance. Diskin and the Colonel, who was Eddy's manager, would be in town for a few days. They were looking for a new rock star to promote and asked if I knew of anyone who might fit the bill.

I immediately thought of **Tommy Sands**, who in addition to his Saturday morning radio show was singing at a raunchy club in Houston's Market Square downtown historic district...Cook's Hoedown. I took Tommy Diskin and Colonel Parker to hear him. I had never been to the club before. They had a small band, and a smaller dance floor. Tommy Diskin asked me to dance and because he was quite a bit shorter than I, I removed my high heels and hit the floor. But not for long. Cook's Hoedown may have been raunchy, but it did have it's rules and shoes required on the dance floor was one of them. I was mortified at being kicked off the dance floor at Cook's Hoedown.

Colonel Parker was immediately impressed with Tommy Sands and wanted to bring him to Hollywood and plan a big buildup for him because "the time was right for a rock and roll superstar". Sands and his mom came to talk it over with me and we all agreed that the move would be a good thing and that Tommy should go for it.

However, shortly thereafter, the two starmakers ran across an even better candidate - **Elvis Presley**. Their plans for Tommy Sands made a sort of U-turn. Colonel Parker and Elvis, however, recommended Tommy for a television special *The Singing Idol*, depicting the life of a fictional rock star which was originally intended for Elvis who was too busy to do it.

Soon after, Sands married Nancy Sinatra, was featured in a few movies, made some top charting records but became discouraged with his career and moved to Hawaii. I tried to locate him in 2005. I had seen him on a *This Is Your Life* broadcast in the '60s, but nobody mentioned me. Guess they forgot who started it all. Last I heard, Sands had relocated to California in late 2005 and later returned to Hawaii. He never remarried after Nancy Sinatra, but has a daughter, Jessica, from a later relationship who is following in her father's musical footsteps. They appeared together at a 2007 Elvis Birthday Bash in Hollywood. At 69, Sands still sings at a few clubs and has never really lost his boyish charm.

I didn't hear much from Tommy Diskin after that, but when I told him that I was going to marry my photo teacher he and the Colonel sent us a wall clock. I don't think I appreciated its value at the time. Through the years, Tommy always sent Christmas cards from Elvis but I did not see him again until a few years later when I was in Los Angeles. We met for dinner. I had no idea that he would become a tycoon not only in the entertainment world, but as a real estate genius dealing in valuable Tennessee property. He married rather late in life and had a lovely daughter. He included her picture in his Christmas greetings. He also sent us cards from Elvis, which I wish I had kept.

We continued exchanging Christmas cards, but in the mid-90's I didn't receive any back from Tom Diskin. Still, I sent cards until 2004. It wasn't until I started writing this book and contacted his nephew, Ed Bonje, that I learned Diskin had been killed in a tragic car accident. How ironic that he and his longtime friend Al Dvorin, would go the same way. And what is even more ironic, Al was a passenger in the car Bonje was driving when it spun out of a curve and rolled down a hill. Al was not wearing a seat belt but Bonje was and although badly injured recovered and is back on the road as a guitar playing singer.

I also learned more about Colonel Parker. He was originally from Amsterdam, Holland; was not a military Colonel but rather a southern colonel, and was a former dog catcher for the Tampa, Florida Humane Society. Always creative, it was reputed, Parker would gather pups from three or four dogs, put them with one Mom, and call the Tampa Tribune to cover the multi-birth phenomena. He was so convincing that he almost always got coverage, according to the Tampa Bay Legends. The illustrious Colonel Parker died from a stroke in 1997.

Back to the early 50s and Fred (Mr. Hollywood) Nahas. He decided that the station needed its own photographer to shoot him with the stars who appeared on Saturday at the Shamrock. Since the show didn't end until 10:00pm, most of the regular photographers were busy with other assignments. So, I volunteered. The station bought me a huge Crown Graphic camera, signed me up for photo-journalism classes at the

University of Houston and rented a small apartment with a kitchen that could be converted into a dark room.

I was assigned a student-teacher at the University of Houston who taught me to stand my subjects six feet from the wall...and shoot! Wasn't easy balancing a huge Crown Graphic camera, flash gun, changing film holders, removing the slide backing. Nothing like today's instant digital. I already mentioned one of my first assignments on the football field. After that, it was a piece of cake most of the time. Except when I forgot to pull the slide when shooting stars like Georgie Jessel and Sophie Tucker and wound up with NO IMAGE!

One thing about having your own darkroom and working with big negatives, you could "burn" an image from almost nothing which I had to do many times. Some of the photos went to the print media for publicity, but ALL of them were framed for Fred's office wall. He was in ALL of them. I gave my collection to the Houston Heritage Society.

It was like going back to my Hy-Shopper days, except I didn't do interviews; just photographed the Saturday at the Shamrock celebrity guests with Fred and Glenn who always sort of hid near the wall of the giant Emerald Room where the show was broadcast.

McCarthy was quiet, almost sullen, most of the time (remember James Dean in *Giant*), sometimes flashing a half smile in recognition of me; sometimes didn't seem to know me at all.

Later, his empire began to crumble. He lost his oil wells, the hotel, the station, the newspapers and much of his dignity. Then, instead of looking through me, he would shout *hello* from the other side of the street and tell me about the jam his wife, Faustine, was making. His only salvation was the moving of his beloved Cork Club from the Shamrock Hotel to the top floor of the Central National Bank Building in the 1960s. At the same time his friend, advertising/health club tycoon Richard L. (Dick) Minns opened his first President's Health Club on the first floor of the same building.

Who guested on the Saturday at the Shamrock radio show? The list was endless. Sophie Tucker, Georgie Jessel, Margaret Whiting, Patti Page, Danny Kaye, Humphrey Bogart, George Burns and Gracie Allen, Dorothy Lamour, Eddie Bracken, Jack Benny, Mel Torme, Dorothy Shay (the Park Avenue Hillbillie)...more than a hundred top rated stars and bandleaders bantered back and forth with Fred on Saturday at the Shamrock.

Audio historian and Nahas' good friend Henry Kjellander captured more than 100 of the original Saturday at the Shamrock broadcasts on tape copied from acetate and aluminum disks made by KXYZ and scattered among junk dealers across the city after the station closed. He found and copied some of them; the rest are lost forever. An important part of Houston's history, Saturday at the Shamrock tapes are still available from Kjellander's Audio Archives, Inc.

McCarthy sold his Shamrock Hotel to the Hilton chain in the '50s which operated it as the Shamrock-Hilton until 1985 when they sold it to the Texas Medical Center. Thus began the demise of Glenn McCarthy's world-renowned Shamrock, the hotel that put Houston on the map and on the road to growth and success was being reduced to a parking lot. Built to last a hundred years, it took eighteen months of wrecking balls to bring the Shamrock down to rubble with its remains still housed in its basement. The super-sized swimming pool, one of the world's largest hotel pools, is now covered over by an expensive parking lot. Sad but true!

McCarthy attended some of the closing public events organized by his friends to salute the Shamrock, but he began refusing his medication when the demolition was complete. One year later, on December 26, 1987. he died, a lonely nearly forgotten man.

Working at KXYZ was a remarkable experience. I got to meet and work with great journalists like Houston Chronicle TV editor Ann Hodges, society columnist Betty Ewing, food editor Beverly Harris (later Lifestyle editor), Houston Press food editor Ann Valentine who is still a good friend and Ben Kaplan, political reporter for the Houston Press.

Kaplan was quite an imbiber and when I volunteered to count election votes at the courthouse, he sat next to me. Little did I realize when he whispered *wanna sip* that he was referring to the booze in his hip flask. We were both asked to leave, even though I never touched the stuff.

My favorite thing was to invite the ladies of the press to lunch at Maxim's across the street from the station in those days. When I returned to Houston several years later, I continued to peddle my *good news* to them and invite them to all of my press functions. Many of them are still around today and still contributing to the world of journalism

KXYZ was a key instigator of Downtown Houston Promotion Days which included a Main Street parade. I thought it would be great to get a flat bed truck and put the Arthur Murray dancers on it to demonstrate their agility, sort of a rolling Dancing with the Stars with a KXYZ banner on the side. The truck started down the street, music blaring, feet twirling, onlookers clapping. Then the truck hit a bump in the road...and they all came tumbling down. I left Houston shortly thereafter, but I don't think they did a repeat performance the following year.

The station had an unusual marketing component headed by Art Stone. He worked with advertisers to get their products prominently displayed with special promotions in retail stores. Stone always made the display arrangements with the stores; I created the promotions that went along with them. One of those clients was Pepsi-Cola. It was the time of the Pepsi/Coca-Cola war, and Pepsi wanted something that would attract youngsters and their parents to the stores to buy Pepsi-Cola. And so, the Pepsi Moon Man was born.

I had recently seen the musical *Lilli* at Houston's Little Theater with a very talented dwarf, Reed Robinson, who sang, danced and had a trained dog act. Tying in with the times, I saw him in a space suit with helmet...The Pepsi Moon Man. I contacted Robinson and he was really excited about the plan. We went to a local costume shop and found a jumpsuit which they dyed silver and created a big round see-thru plastic space helmet.

Our first appearance was at one of the grocery chains. Robinson showed up in his moon man outfit with a couple of the dogs and talked to the children who were fascinated by him while a Pepsi rep poured free samples of the drink. We made a couple of store appearances before our big gig...a major car dealer which would attract a broader audience. We broke the full act in at a small car dealership which was having an anniversary celebration with a large flatbed truck converted to a stage. Arriving with five overactive dogs, we had to wait for a country music act to finish before we could go on.

The dogs became increasingly impatient and Reed was having difficulty controlling them. Finally, it was his turn onstage. He hauled the dogs to the platform, explaining to the audience what the dogs were going to do. He didn't expect what they were really going to do...relieve themselves all over the stage. Reed tried to stay cool and continue talking to the audience while slipping and sliding on poop all over the stage. It was a disaster.

Our final performance was at a major car dealership. To peak excitement, it was advertised that the Pepsi Moon Man would arrive by helicopter at the side entrance to the dealership. Hundreds of people were gathered to greet the Moon Man as he descended to the ground. The chopper door opened and this seemingly disoriented dwarf stepped out, swerving and...exposed. Robinson had never ridden in a helicopter before, got air sick, unzipped his space suit, and forgot to re-zip. There he was in all of his glory; the young audience didn't seem to notice, but the dealership owner did. That was the Pepsi Moon Man's last appearance.

Fred retired from the radio business, worked for an advertising agency and then opened his own agency with partner Eddie Bracken.

Later photos of Fred showed him as a Bracken look-alike. Fred passed away in 1994. KXYZ is now a Mexican music station.

I married my student photography teacher in 1952, Leland Lavere (Lee) Estes worked for the Houston Chronicle as an assistant art critic and police reporter (great combination) while at the University of Houston.

Since he was in ROTC at the University of Houston, we went into the Army right after graduation and moved to Fort Sam Houston in San Antonio, Texas.

Being a wife was new enough to me, but being an Army wife was a complete shock. Quartered on the base at Infantry Post Loop at Fort Sam Houston, the apartment was boring but clean...very clean. It was the first time I had witnessed the *white glove inspection.* Going in wasn't so bad, but moving out was a nightmare.

After getting settled, I went on a job search and was successful at the San Antonio Chamber of Commerce. They hired me on a temporary basis to hype up the city's Vegetable Day celebration which had been losing momentum for years.

I came up with a plan for recipe contests and a Miss Vegetable Day competition for vegetable farmers daughters or other relatives. Hattie Lewelyn, then food editor of the now defunct San Antonio Light, was most helpful and agreed to promote the event. Food editor of the Express-News also participated which was most unusual since, historically, competing newspapers did not do joint promotions. But I promised to deliver different material to each and pointed out that each had its own readership. Besides it was for the good of the vegetable growers and San Antonio. After four weeks of soliciting recipes, the best ones were printed in each paper. The grand prize winner, selected by Hattie Lewellyn, was an eggplant dish.

Ace photographer Jimmy Zintgraf and I went out to the winner's farm where she greeted us with smiles and lemonade. After several minutes, I mentioned that we should probably get started with the photo, just as soon as the egg plants were on the counter. Jimmy and the winner just stared. Several bright purple egg plants were already there. Actually, I had never seen an eggplant before and was looking for something small and white... like an egg.

Jeanette Van De Walle, of the famed Van De Walle Farms family (later changed to San Antonio Farms becoming famous for Piquante Sauce ultimately purchased by Campbell Soups) was San Antonio's first Vegetable Day Queen. She was one of ten siblings. I remember having dinner there was like sitting down at the Last Supper twelve people at one of the biggest tables I had ever seen. Imagine cooking for twelve people three times a day...every day. WOW!

My next assignment with the Chamber was assisting advertising-PR exec Jim Battersby, then with Pitluk Advertising, in promoting the San Antonio Livestock

Show & Rodeo. Again, I got to partner with Zintgraff. Our first assignment was to cover a high school class studying grasses for a rodeo grass judging competition. When we arrived, several boys were at the blackboard writing the names of the grasses that the teacher held up. Deciding on a setup, I looked at the board and noticed Sweet Sudan (a grass). Not knowing the students, I naively asked. "Which one of you boys is sweet?" Needless to say, it brought down the house.

Our next assignment was to shoot some prized steers which would be entered in the stock show competition. Being a city girl, I didn't know the difference between a steer and a bull and neither did Jimmy. Once we found out, we spent the afternoon with our heads down checking out animals' undersides. The rancher couldn't believe us. Still don't know how you tell a bull from a steer by looking him straight in the eye.

During rodeo time, I was obviously pregnant, as was a cow in the competition. Battersby took bets on which would foal first. Fortunately, I lost. My days in San Antonio were numbered, however, because we were assigned to Aschaffenburg Germany, a small city about forty miles outside of Frankfurt. I was scheduled to leave right after the Rodeo. Husband left first. I followed.

Glen McCarthy's Shamrock Hotel...in the beginning...now gone forever.

Singer Tommy Sands with country favorite Ernie Ford.

Colonel Tom Parker (second left), KXYZ's "Mr.Hollywood" Fred Nahas, Me, and Tommy Diskin at Saturday at the Shamrock.

Hamming it up, teenaged Tommy Sands posed with Colonel Parker and two of his employees.

Tommy Sands...more recently.

Saturday at the Shamrock crooner Dick Krueger.

Larry Hovis as a TV star on Hogan's Heroes.

You win! KXYZ announcer Tim Nolan, right, and sports director Guy Savage, left, present prizes to a lucky contest winner.

Behind the feathers, Georgie Jessel, renowned columnist Hedda Happer, a Houston socialite and a pilot celebrate the Shamrock Hotel's opening in the Cork Club.

Moving day for the San Antonio Rodeo office - 1952.

I was enlisted as a catchall for a San Antonio accessories show.

The Four Spades: Harry, Larry, Joe and Jerry were regulars on KXYZ.

CHAPTER 4

Missing Elvis in Frankfurt

Although my heritage was German on my mother's side, the only German word I knew was Gesundtheit (God bless you!). Leaving San Antonio, just a few weeks before our first-born was expected was scary, but I got through the flight from hell none the worse for the experience.

This book was not planned to be about me, but I couldn't resist including some of the personal stuff. The trip to Germany was unbelievable. The plane left San Antonio early in the evening and arrived in New York early the next morning, pretty much as scheduled. Takeoff in early afternoon to Germany was also on time, so everything was cool...I thought.

Several hours later, we landed – in Germany, I thought. Wrong. The sign said *Welcome to Boston!* Seems the plane had an engine problem but the pilot did not want to worry the passengers, so he kept flying in circles before deciding to turn back. It was near midnight when we arrived at the Boston airport.

Restaurants were closed so there was no food and passengers were told that it would take a few hours to get a new plane ready for flight, offering the option of an overnight hotel stay, or free drink tickets until the plane was ready to take off, saving a couple of hours time. The majority ruled. Drink tickets won out. It was now going on two days since I had left San Antonio and I was still in the same clothes. I felt scummy.

Finally taking off again, we landed in New York with a few hours wait for the next plane to Germany. Taking advantage of the time lapse, I noticed that showers were offered in the ladies' restroom for 25 cents. I took advantage of the opportunity, dropped my quarter in the slot and proceeded to disrobe and step into the shower.

The water automatically turned off in just a couple of seconds and there I was; pregnant, stripped naked and drippy with no more quarters. Naturally, I thought towels were provided. Wrong again. The next several minutes were spent blotting my dripping body with paper towels.

Next and only stop on the itinerary was Greenland, The weather was terrible and the plane rocked and rolled hitting deep air pockets. I kept my eye on the little brown bag in the seat pocket in front of me; just in case my old friend motion sickness came back. Fortunately, I was okay. It was freezing in Greenland, but this time, the plane took off on time. Next stop, Frankfurt, West Germany...more than a day late.

Landing at the airport, I couldn't wait to find my husband -- who wasn't there. He had been there and back a couple of times waiting for the plane, then returned to his post in Aschaffenburg. Finally, what seemed to be a lifetime, I spotted him wearing a Tyrolean hat trying to look like a native.

We got into the car and proceeded to drive. It was very very dark. And we drove and drove and drove until I finally asked, "Well, how far is it?"

At about this time, we saw a light and a bunch of guards in unfamiliar uniforms coming toward us, guns pointed. By mistake, my husband had taken us over the Russian border into the occupied zone.

Retracing the route, we finally arrived in Aschaffenburg, located on the edge of Bavaria. Our new home, a rundown old house that was even spookier inside than out with huge animal antlers lining the staircase and on all of the walls. Frau Bach, the crochety old landlady, was an avid hunter and basked in advertising her successes.

The next surprise. The tiny one-and-half rooms had NO heat, NO bath and NO water. I couldn't believe it. There was a bath in the hallway. The hot water tank took lots of d-marks; but it didn't work.

Thoughtful husband announced that he was going back to the BOQ (bachelor officers quarters) to take a shower and I was left to freeze...dirty and still very pregnant. We finally rented a propane gas cook stove and used it as a heater. The pot bellied stove in the living room was a complete loss; I flunked Girl Scout campfire building.

Looking back, it really wasn't all that bad. Aschaffenburg was a city with a heart and the caring ladies of the town took pity on me. They thought all Americans were rich and lived in fancy houses. By that standard, I was at the bottom of the barrel. They all had it better than I did and so, they took me under their wings.

Veteran officers' wives were not quite so kind, but they did allow me to join their canasta club (I hate card games!). However, I went to the weekly sessions armed with soap and towel to take a shower. They all lived in the big regulation Army quarters with all the niceties of life...like heat and hot water. Since we started out as short termers, we were not afforded the same luxury.

Just before our first born, Victoria Marie, arrived we upgraded our quarters, but not much. A solid concrete structure with six damp separate 8 x 10 rooms, each opening onto a hallway with a community bath at the end was being built nearby. It was originally intended for six single officers who did not want to live on base, but the builder agreed to rent to two second lieutenant families; three rooms each. We shared with 2nd Lt. Robert Carder, his wife Shirley and their new baby boy, David from Norman, Oklahoma. At least it was better than Frau Bach's and there was a water heater - if you knew how to build a wood fire. I still didn't.

Settled for the time being, I found a kinderschwester (baby nurse) and went job hunting, landing a free-lance post with Stars & Stripes. I covered special events and general news in Aschaffenburg, which wasn't much. The small city with two of "Crazy" King Ludwig's castles was the center for manufacture of men's clothing and I became friends with the daughter of one of the best known companies. She helped me find story material and took me on exciting excursions to Frankfurt to shop and have coffee at Cafe Krantzler's, an elegant spot with great desserts and quiet music.

Town photographers Helmet and Margot Streiter also became close friends. Helmut would pick me up on his motorscooter and take me to town shopping. On one of the couple's scooter trips, an out-of-control car slammed into them and totally shattered Margot's face. I remember going to the hospital to cheer her up with friend husband who took one look at her and passed out on the floor. Hospital personnel scattered around removing him from the room and Margot...I don't think she ever got over that. Needless to say, she certainly wasn't *cheered.*

Aschaffenburg translates to "castle at the ash tree river", referring to the Aschaff river that runs through parts of the town. The original Schloss (castle) was built by the Frankish mayors in 1122. After many catastrophes including war and fire the schloss was reconstructed by Archbishop Johann Schweikard von Kronberg (1604-1626). It survived the Thirty Years War however, the chapel is the only structure that has remained pretty much in tact.

Across the river from the main castle is the Pompeiianum, built by King Ludwig I (1840-48).

Situated high above the Main River, the only access to the second story was from the roof. Practically every day I strolled on the grounds with our new baby Victoria in her royal European carriage reliving the tales the town ladies told me.

Whether true or not, they said that King Ludwig, known as the crazy king, lived in the main castle across the river and kept his paramour Lola Montez in the "little castle". The story goes that he would hold a candle up to a mirror which reflected in a mirror at the Pompeiianum signaling to his lover that he was on his way through an underground passage.

May not be true, but it was very romantic and fun to think about .The main castle had been badly damaged in World War II and trained artisans were in the process of restoring it when we left in the mid-50s. In a 1980's visit, I found the castle restored and converted into an art museum and restaurant. Now it's commercial rather than romantic.

Deciding to extend our tour of duty, husband landed a spot in Frankfurt, and we prepared to move to civilized digs like the rest of the officers. First in a private apartment, then to an army community, and finally, to a great three-story German house with a back yard for Viki and our soon-expected second daughter, Lorilei Elaine, named for the mystic maiden on the rock on the Rhine River.

Job hunting in Frankfurt was a snap. I continued with Starts & Stripes and found The Overseas Weekly newspaper (commonly known as The ***Oversexed Weekly*** because of its sexy cover shots and content) with headquarters at the Frankfurt Press Club. I signed on as a free lance feature writer doing mostly women's stuff. The only stars I saw in those days were in the sky and a few celebrities who came to the Press Club.

One day, while reading proofs at the printer in downtown Frankfurt, I ran across a magazine with a sleek checkerboard cover. ***Made in Europe*** was aimed at retailers in the states. It covered products *made in Europe*, but designed for North American "good taste" like musical coffee grinders that, instead of grinding coffee, played the Tennessee Waltz.

I walked over to the office, which was near the printer in downtown Frankfurt, and was hired on the spot as an associate editor and circulation manager (to justify my wages). I was probably one of the few Americans working for D-marks on the German economy. My assignments included covering trade fairs in Germany, Italy, Spain and Switzerland and writing feature articles. It was a dream job and I ran into a few *semi* stars. Yves Pontevant was the president of the European Productivity Association (EPA), the first signs of a unified Europe and we went to France to interview him.

I spent almost four years with Made in Europe and had a fantastic time. **Herman Reisner**, the publisher, came from Berlin where he and his uncle published the Ubersee Post, a popular weekly business newspaper. During the war, he moved to Frankfurt and started his own publication. Made in Europe is still being published but has an entirely different look and content...mostly business.

Other *stars* were manufacturers of great products that were advertised in the magazine. Most of the advertisers were very happy with the exposure to the states, all except one. They made foam rubber sandals with gaudy flowers. Woolworth's loved them and ordered 100 dozen. The advertiser came to Frankfurt seething. They couldn't produce that many sandals in a lifetime, much less in a few weeks to fill the Woolworth order. To each his own.

I met internationally acclaimed Dutch architect and industrial designer **Jaap Penraat** and his fiber artist wife, Jetty on an assignment in Holland. The magazine sent me to Amsterdam to interview him and do an article on his modern design line of birch and beech do-it-yourself furniture that Herr Reisner thought would do well on the U.S. market. The Penraats graciously put me up in their three-story town house (which I later tried to imitate in Houston), fed me and told me fascinating stories about their experiences with the dreaded Nazis. Jetty was pregnant while Amsterdam was occupied and couldn't get to a hospital. She finally found a bike and cycled her way through deserted streets arriving at the hospital just in time.

Since I would be returning stateside in a few months, Penraat suggested that he send me some samples of his furniture for presentation to major retailers in the states. I eventually made a deal with Foley's in downtown Houston to display the line which was very contemporary, very easy too put together and made of birch and beech wood to last.

As a matter of fact, more than forty years later, I still have some pieces that are in good shape. Unfortunately, the line did not catch on. Americans were getting lazy. They didn't want to *do it themselves* anymore.

Only after starting this book did I learn how really important Jaap Penraat was. According to an article published in the Industrial Design Society of America newsletter (IDSA) excerpted from *DESIGN CHRONICLES - Significant Mass-produced \Designs of the 20th Century* by Carroll M. Gantz, FIDSA, published in 2005 by Schiffer Publications, Ltd.), did I learn that Penraat was an international hero.

A non-Jew trained as an architect and designer in Amsterdam, he joined the Dutch resistance during the 1940-45 Nazi occupation of Holland in World War II when Dutch Jews were persecuted. He forged fake identity cards for Jews, was discovered by the Nazis and sent to prison for several months. He was tortured but remained silent about his operations. After his release, he forged fake travel papers for Jews disguised as construction workers for Hitler's Atlantic Wall in France. He personally escorted over 400 of them, in groups of twenty, to safety in Spain. After 1944, the trips became too risky and he hid in a remote Dutch village, subsisting on sugar beets.

Seems that in 1958. shortly after I returned to America, he brought his family including Jetty and their three children to New York to design a Dutch Mill cafe for the 1964 New York World's Fair and settled in the Catskills. He continued designing contemporary furniture and was a featured speaker at many ASID/IDI/IDSA meetings.

And here's where the REAL STAR emerged. In the early 1970's, Penraat got involved in the film industry and was co- producer/director with Jack Deveau of the 1972 film, *Left-Handed* with a cast that included Sal Mineo. Penraat also performed as an actor in *Drive* and *Adam & Yves,* both directed by Deveau in 1974. His daughter, Noelle, became a noted filmographer described as, "the best negative cutter in the film business."

Although he refused for many years to talk about his wartime experiences, according to the IDSA article, his daughter Noel encouraged him to make his deeds public and speak about them at school and civic group meetings. In 1981, Penraat was awarded a war pension by the Dutch government. He received the *verzetsherdenkingkrius* (Cross of Resistance) in 1994 as *Righteous Among the Nations* from Yad Vashem, which is Israel's official memorial to victims of the Holocaust. He was also added to its honor roll in Jerusalem. Jaap Penraat passed away in June 2006. So you see, one never knows when or where a star will show up.

Another *star* I ran across, was Ann Maness, originally from France. She wanted to open a boutique in downtown Frankfurt but couldn't afford the high rents for most of the places. She finally settled on a vacant telephone booth, about 4 x 6 feet in size. Just 24 square feet, it was not your everyday boutique. She put in a little counter and hung designer originals around the perimeter. If she didn't have your size, she could order it. When someone wanted to try on a garment patrons were escorted outside and the curtained folding door was closed.

Wanting to learn the German language better, I enrolled at Goethe University, Germany's center for finance and economic studies. I spent two years there taking a Kurs fur Auslandern (course for foreigners) and had a splendid time. Most of the students came from all over Europe and the middle east. No one spoke the same language so, as a group, we learned German really fast together, practicing over dinner and cocktails.

About the same time, Elvis Presley joined the Army and was stationed in Germany. I never got to meet him there, or anywhere else for that matter. And I never saw the Colonel again either.

A bonus job came along when Compass News Service, a London, England public relations firm, hired me to work with their Sudanese cotton fabric fashion shows. They had just acquired Sudan and wanted to publicize the cotton by giving free fabric to well known European designers who created for fashion shows at some of the trade shows I covered. The *modern production* system touted was actually scantily clad natives stomping on the cotton bolls. Needless to say the sleek designer fashions displayed on the runway didn't reveal how the cotton was actually produced. But the final product was amazing.

Covering a trade fair in Milan, I learned a lot of patience! Scheduled to open on Thursday and close on Sunday, I arrived for the Thursday opening. Practically none of the booths were set up. By Friday, stragglers rolled in setting up spaces and drinking coffee and wine. By Saturday, the show was about to begin. On Sunday, dismantling began. Very difficult to cover except for the Japanese who were ahead of the game with wrist watch cameras enabling them to shoot a new product and come back with it in their own space practically overnight.

Having to photograph some of the items for my article, I looked for a shop to buy film and asked a passerby if he knew of one. A roly-poly twinkly eyed man agreed to lead us to a shop and then offered to take us to the opera at La Scala that night. Husband and I were thrilled. He said he was a dethroned Italian count. We agreed to meet him in front of La Scala at seven.

When we got there, he was waiting. And that's what we all did. Wait. Finally, I asked when we were going in. He informed us that we were there just to watch the people go in. We were going to watch the opera on TV at his friend's pub. The television there didn't work, but the evening wasn't wasted. We did get to see who can afford to attend La Scala in Milan.

Assigned to cover the opening the of the Galeria, Barcelona's first covered shopping mall, I got another taste of patience. Make a date in Spain and you are at the mercy of a myriad of conflicting activities that will postpone the meeting. Weddings, funerals, birthdays, rest... anything can interfere with being on time in Barcelona.

Eventually, I got my story and was rewarded with a side trip to Mallorica, a true paradise if ever there was one. My friend, Nurry Vandelos from the Overseas Weekly, had a grandmother who lived there and I immediately wanted to buy a house there, too. I was talked out of it because of a serious water shortage there, to say nothing of the long trek back and forth from the states on a low income budget.

Time was running out on this splendid tour of duty in Germany with maids and baby sitters and wine and fun jobs. It was time to return to the land of reality...Houston, Texas. Bummer!

Aschaffenburg...the home of King Ludwig

Fraulein Viki – 2 years old

Stifkirche – Aschaffenburg

Yaap Penraat – Hero and Creator

CHAPTER 5

George H. W. Bush – Off to Congress

Back in Houston, we found a small, but brand new house between Galveston and downtown. I settled in with my two girls and a couple of cats while husband completed his tour of duty in Virginia. It's not easy going from the lap of luxury to a suburb with no car (couldn't drive then anyway), no babysitter and only a gas station Quik Stop close enough to walk to with two toddlers in a wagon.

We did bring home a tiny iso Isetta, just 4.5 feet wide and 7.5 feet long, with a single door that opened from the front with the steering wheel attached, rear wheels just 19 inches apart and gas mileage over 50 miles per gallon. If you're old enough to remember, Fred Astaire drove one in *Funny Face* with Kay Thompson seeking out Audrey Hepburn in Paris

It had a fold back top, three-speed shift, a top speed of 45mph and propulsion up to 30 mph in 36 seconds meaning that getting onto a Houston freeway was a near death wish. All you could do was look very carefully, close your eyes, pray and head into the traffic. I practiced driving until I could do it well enough to go for a license. Even then, I still had trouble parking. Once it broke down it was impossible to find parts so the Isetta had to be trashed.

Instead of looking for a job, I decided to open my own business based on the Made In Europe concept of *healthy international trade leads to international peace.* Named Zestes International with a sputnic-zooming-around-the- world logo, I designed stationery, promotion pieces and went about peddling my European finds: Penraat's furniture, authentic German dirndls, china, crystal and a few other items. At the same time, we welcomed our son Erik into the world. To save on babysitting, he would accompany me to the small office I found, kept safe in his tiny basket.

Houston wasn't much interested in international trade at that time, so I had the financial obligation to find a real job. It seems they were planning a Foreign Trade Center in the warehouse part of town and needed a promotion person. Just my cup of tea.

I applied and got the job immediately. The salary was great and the concept even greater. Dedicated to the petroleum industry, the "showroom" would include some of the nation's biggest and best oil field equipment which was to be displayed in the huge warehouse space. One or two multi-lingual sales people were hired to represent all of the companies. Buyers from around the world were invited to view and buy the equipment at a one-stop shop and enjoy lunch and a drink at the glamorous Foreign Trade Club.

Austrian citizen Ingeborg Killeen and her American partner/lover Bill (can't remember his last name) sold Houston a real bill of goods, and I backed them up with outstanding publicity and public relations. Our final event was a giant international Christmas party to be held at the club and televised live on KPRC-TV (NBC).

Children from every country were invited and the celebration was crowned with pinatas, a visit from St. Nicholaus who rewarded the good with gifts and his evil opponent Krampus, the devil, who carried a whip. I remember my youngest daughter, Lori, running and crying, "Don't get me. I never done nothing bad."

Unfortunately, Ingeborg and Bill DID do something bad. They took all of the project's investments and skipped the country. It was a disaster. All salary checks bounced; the food and beverage purveyors didn't get paid and one of the sales staff, who had been recently released from mental rehab was returned for treatment.

My remembrance is a pair of metal fighting cocks and a camphor wood mask. I don't think Houston has ever attempted a Foreign trade Center since.

Popular Houston radio celebrity Ted Nabors had a small advertising agency with Downey Brothers build-on-your-lot homes as his major account. I joined him and wrote, designed and placed all of the advertising and publicity for them and got settled back into what I knew best. Writing in English!

From Nabors, I moved to S. L. Brown & Associates. Sylvan Brown was a rather short man married to an even shorter wife, Lavonne (he called Von). He had served in the U.S. Navy during World War II and opened his advertising agency in 1958, becoming a pioneer in creating classy television commercials.

My media contacts came in handy here since S.L. concentrated on the paid advertising side of the business while I was always looking for the "freebies"...radio and television interviews and print articles. One of my favorite radio shows to bring guests was a talk show on KTRH-Houston with hosts Thelma Schoettker and Steve Edwards. The pair were so compatible and always seemed to bring out the best in their guests. They had a very loyal audience and were so easy to work with.

Edwards left KTRH to go to Hollywood where he hosted a talk show with Connie Chung, a pre-Regis and Kelly talk show and a variety of other talk shows. Edwards received a star on the Hollywood Walk of Fame in 2004 and continues to host top-rated news and talk shows.

Thelma Schoettker went on to have her own talk show on KPRC-TV, write many specials for public television and works free lance with veteran newsman Dan Ammerman, chairman and CEO of The Ammerman Experience, a pioneer in the media training industry. An accomplished broadcaster, Ammerman has appeared in many television movies and shows including the hit series, Dallas.

Shoettker moved back to her native Cincinnati, Ohio several years ago, and still works with Ammerman. Some of my fondest Thelma memories were the small gatherings of local semi-celebrities at her apartment. Theatrical publicist Jonni Hartman, mother of **Lisa Hartman,** was one of her best friends. It was at one of these gatherings that Jonni announced that she was taking her not-quite-teenaged daughter, Lisa, to

Hollywood. Lisa was less than happy about her mom's decision. Her dad, Howard Hartman was a popular lounge singer in Houston and Lisa had inherited his musical talent.

As a teenager, she also fronted some local rock bands and reluctantly sang a number for a media gathering at the Houston Press Club. I think she was about sixteen when she went on the road with a motorcycle daredevil who was performing at the Houston Astrodome. Watching her blossom into a true star of records, television and movies was really exciting.

I think her marriage to Clint Black was the best thing that could have ever happened. They were at last able to turn away from the spotlight to a happy peaceful personal life. Jonni was Black's assistant for a time, but eventually, Lisa and Clint were again free from parental pressures and were able to concentrate on their own parenting skills with daughter Lilly Pearl.

Sylvan Brown had a dry, wry sense of humor that was infectious. He could take the simplest tale and turn it into a comedy that would have you in stitches. He also liked to down a few before going home after a long late day of creativity at the office.

Since he lived in the trendy Memorial section of Houston which was like the country in those days (mid-50s), he had to conquer many sharp curves on the way home and always seemed to miss one and wind up in a ditch. He would then call his favorite tow service which was familiar with his habitual mishap. They would come tow him out and in no time, he would be back on his way.

Another traffic mishap. Because he felt a little sleepy late one night, Sylvan parked in the middle lane of a busy downtown Houston street and turned off the motor for a short snooze. Some time later, when a policeman tapped on the window, Sylvan was awakened and escorted to jail.

He explained to the judge that he had been told when he felt sleepy in the car, he should pull over and take a nap. But not in the middle of the street, the judge reprimanded.

He was found guilty and given a fine. But, with no cash in his pocket, Sylvan cheerfully offered to pay with a credit card and displayed his collection (not acceptable at that time). The judge had no sense of humor and threw Sylvan in the clink until next morning when his attorney came to rescue him.

I met my first president at S. L. Brown's in 1963. **George H. W. Bush** was running for Congress and chose Sylvan Brown to create a campaign image for him. The result: huge billboards depicting Bush with his jacket casually thrown over one shoulder to characterize him as a regular guy with a down-to-earth approach to politics, even though he was already a millionaire as co-owner of Zapata Oil.

Bush and wife Barbara came to the office a couple of times during the campaign to approve news releases and go over Brown's advertising plans for the campaign. Bush won the race to Congress, moved to Washington and was on his way to his eventual ultimate success - president of the United States. In the meantime, he was appointed ambassador to the United nations (1971-3) when again I got to work with him as he hosted United Nations birthday parties. In 1990, I was a media representative at his Economic Summit of Industrial Nations in Houston.

Putting **Shearn Smith** into a Judge's seat was not quite so easy. A prominent attorney and University of Houston alumnus, Smith was a strong family man, religious, righteous and all of those things good for politicians. His biggest plus was that the kind of activities he was involved with generated genuine news. He took his sons on exotic Boy Scout camping trips, led unique fund raising campaigns for his church and was a leader in the UH alumni community. But he had lots of competitors trying to dig up the dirt on him so we had to always be on our guard.

As a part of his campaign we planned to have him speak at a U of H alumni dinner. That, in itself, is not very newsy. But remembering Shasta, the friendly U of H cougar mascot we had worked with for a television commercial, we decided to bring the tame cat to dinner in a red Radio Flyer wagon which Smith was donating to the university. In the past, students had to carry Shasta in his cage out onto the field. Now he would have his own wheels.

We pulled him onto the floor of the spacious hotel banquet room in his little red wagon, past the goodie laden buffet table. Then, Shasta took a detour out of the wagon and back to the buffet table. It was utter chaos, but it made the news.

Going back to his successful *George Bush for Congress* campaign, Sylvan created a series of ads and billboards depicting Smith in a judge's robe in the courtroom at the "bench" with a gavel. The copy: Vote for JUDGE SHEARN SMITH, gave the impression he already was a judge. Who noticed the tiny "for"?

It worked. Judge Shearn Smith served on the bench in a Houston courtroom until his retirement in 1996. His pet project, jury selection reform, attracted national recognition and he continued to update the process throughout his career.

The only other political campaign I worked on for Sylvan was David Gibson, a prominent attorney, who also had his sights on a judge's seat. Sylvan designed a campaign that was catchy, but midway, Gibson decided he did not want to be confined to a judge's bench for the rest of his life. So, he lost and he was free!

Sylvan Brown firmly believed in television advertising and was a genius when it came to creating commercials that sold. Somehow, he managed to switch clients from their traditional print ads to really splashy television productions. He also had fantastic off-the-wall production savvy that was way ahead of its time.

For Battlesteins, a long time family owned Houston fashion emporium, he created a fresh approach featuring young performers in a "musical", much like today's Target series. They were students at Houston's High School for the Performing Arts. His reasoning:

Battlestein's had appealed to the same customers for so many years that they were getting old and dying off. They needed to attract a whole new generation – the teen to thirty set-- if they were going to survive.

Popular ex-model Judy Ward was the store's fashion coordinator and welcomed the new approach. It was a success, but too late to revive Battlestein's faltering image enough to avoid closing. The longtime retailer had served Houston's best for at least three generations. It was a real Houston loss.

It was this same ingenuity that inspired Brown to create such great commercials for other clients specializing in new car sales. To introduce the new Cougar car, we borrowed Shasta, the Cougar mascot from the University of Houston, hired two sexy models, put them in mini mini outfits and thigh high patent leather boots, and headed for the beach. The cougar was unbelievably easy to work with and it was a really pleasant day in the sand. The effort was well worth it. It sold lots of Cougars and won an award for S. L. Brown.

On the cooler side, we handled the Ice Follies when they came to Houston. I remember meeting **Peggy Flemming**, an Olympic medalist, who starred in one of the productions that came to Houston. I interviewed her in her dressing room. She was quietly knitting to pass the time between her skating routines. Taking the U.S.'s only Olympic Gold Medal in 1968, she amazed audiences with her skating routine to the music of Ave Maria.

In 1970, she married dermatologist Dr. Greg Jenkins, a one time ice dance competitor, had two sons and now three grandsons. Fleming was diagnosed with breast cancer in 1998 and has been a champion for the cause ever since. She is also a commentator on figure skating competitions for ABC Sports with fellow Olympics winner Dick Buttons and is a spokesperson for the National Osteoporosis Foundation.

For Dugan Drugs, Brown developed a co-op advertising campaign with its suppliers that, instead of costing money, made a profit through skillful scheduling.

Sylvan Brown also managed to pick up a lot of show business venues in Houston. Probably the most bazaar was the local Holiday Holiday Dinner Theater. **Dean Goss** and his wife Elaine came to us and asked if we could help them promote a dinner theater they were planning to open near the new Astrodome off of South Main street.

Dean already had a reputation as a college football star and was making a name for himself as a comedian, announcer and a bit player in the movies. He had met Elaine on an airplane where she was a hostess and he a passenger. He swept her off her feet, married her and brought her back to Houston.

The *Holiday Dinner Theater* was to feature fine food which Dean, a hulk of a man who loved to eat, would oversee. He would also entertain before and after the main production. The theater was an immediate, if short lived, success with mass appealing shows and fairly good food at a reasonable price.

However, after a few months, business began to slack, as did the payments to S. L. Brown & Associates. So, we dropped the account. But the Gosses continued to seek our advice. They contacted us on what turned out to be their final effort, a New Years Eve special. I can still hear Elaine excitedly explaining their New Years Eve fare: Tobacco Road. "It is a comedy, isn't it?" she gushed. Needless to say, Tobacco flunked as a comedy and that was the end of the Holiday Dinner Theater...but not the end of the Gosses.

Not too many years later, Elaine Goss, a striking woman with flaming red hair, was found murdered in their home under mysterious circumstances, the second of Goss's wives to go that way. Dean claimed no part in the deed and was never charged. To date (2007) the murder has gone unsolved and there is no information on it.

Dean Goss had become involved with Sam Cammarata, an entertainment manager and booking agent with a reputed shady past (and future). Well known in the entertainment business, he was probably responsible for Goss being cast as the police officer in the 1971 film, Brewster McCloud, which was shot almost entirely at the Houston Astrodome. Goss was also a short time announcer for a variety of game shows... *I'm Telling, High Rollers, Bargain Hunters* and *Let's Make a Deal.*

According to news articles, Cammarata was involved in some money laundering, fraud and mismanagement of his clients' money. One of those was rockabilly singer **Ray Frushay** who I worked with a few years later. The Gosses had two sons. One was Dean Jr., now a popular radio disk jockey in California.

At about this time, I was looking for another change. Sylvan Brown had few public relations type accounts and was more interested in electronic media scheduling techniques. He had developed a revolutionary computer program for media scheduling and eventually concentrated on that and dropped the creative side of the agency. Instead, he played a lot of golf.

Isetta – original bug gas saver brought back from Germany.

George H. W. Bush goes to Congress.

Olympic gold medal winner Peggy Flemming performed with the Ice Follies that we promoted in Houston

Participating in a formal Japanese Tea Ceremony at the defunct Houston Foreign Trade Center.

CHAPTER SIX

Richard L. Minns – A Wanted Man

Since I was working by the hour and for an occasional commission, I needed to earn more money. Brown suggested that I contact his former employer, a rather obnoxious but very bright and successful ad man: **Richard L. Minns**, owner of the Richard L. Minns Agency.

He and wife, Mimi, ran the agency with iron fists; he from the sales/creative side; she from the business/ financial end. They were a ruthless combination. Dick started the agency upon graduating from the University of Texas while still working as an ad salesman for the rotogravure section at the Houston Chronicle. He had business cards made up with his agency name...and the Chronicle phone numbers. He had guts!

Minns moved up closer to his dreams of being an advertising tycoon after one of his on-the-side clients, American Health Club, went bankrupt and he sued for the advertising money they owed him. After a long court battle, Minns won. Not cash, but a few of the American Health Club locations.

Typical of his frugal side, he immediately changed the name on the neon signs from AMERICAN HEALTH CLUB to *ACE RICAN,* utilizing the same letters in order to avoid investing in a new sign. After that, he got into the health club business big time and left the security of the Houston Chronicle desk and phone to move into his own space in an old building on Waugh Drive. Ace Rican became his biggest money maker as an investment, selling all sorts of health remedies and club memberships as well as being a substantial advertising account.

Because of his unique creative advertising and marketing style, Minns quickly became a "wanted man" by a wide range of diversified clients. Later he would become one of the FBI's '10 Most Wanted", not for his advertising ability, but for suspicion of a murder-for-hire plot that involved him and a mistress.

Minns hired me as vice-president of public relations in the late fifties replacing a former newspaper reporter who had held the job...with a bottle under his desk. Among the accounts I was expected to promote were Sprague & Carleton Furniture, manufactured in Keene, New Hampshire and owned by Houstonian Sid Laden; New Home Sewing Machines; Blue Ribbon Rice;

Carnation Milk; Kenneth Schnitzer Enterprises, Houston Paper Company, Spare Tire and lots of home builders and developers. They were all mesmerized by Richard's outrageous but most always successful sales pitches and ideas.

We didn't have many *stars* in our stable, but opera singer **Marguerite Piazza** did agree to record a Blue Ribbon Rice Dinner radio commercial. It was the first rice meal-in-a-package on the market. We worked up an aggressive advertising campaign keeping food editors up to date on new recipe ideas using the product. Because the Blue Ribbon dinners were way ahead of their time they went off the market long before Rice-A-Roni and all the other packaged rice dinners arrived on the shelves.

Working with Sprague & Carleton furniture, I traveled a lot hitting the major furniture markets around the country. In New York, we hosted a press party, sending out champagne glasses with an invitation urging the media to come fill them up and view the new Sprague & Carleton line (which was never ready on time). The *star* for Sprague was Melanie Kahane, an internationally recognized interior designer who created sample rooms highlighting Sprague's solid maple early American furniture for press coverage.

Sounds glamorous. Only thing, Richard allowed me just $25 a day for expenses, including hotel and meals which meant that I had to attend other press parties which offered food with a brown bag to pick up and save the snacks. Actually, the only real meal I had was breakfast, because it was the cheapest and most filling.

I usually made my trade show trips alone, but R. L. decided to accompany me on one to Chicago because he liked the city. The experience was unforgettable. It was a cold winter evening and Hugh Hefner's Playboy Club had just opened in downtown Chicago. Naturally, Richard wanted to see it.

When we arrived, there was a long line waiting outside in the cold (market time was always in February, Chicago's coldest month). Of course, Richard thought that everyone should know who he was...Richard L. Minns, health club tycoon, from Houston, Texas!! (They had never heard of him.)

So he cut the line and explained how important he was in Texas. The girls at the entrance were not impressed, just shrugged and went on to the next in line. When his turn finally came up, he reached for his wallet as the girl asked to see his membership card. He didn't have one. So he handed her cash. She refused it.

"Do you know who I am," Richard demanded. "I own a big advertising agency and a string of health clubs, and..."

Nobody cared. But he made such a scene that they finally gave him a card and we were admitted to avoid losing their other customers while he ranted and raved.

Once inside, we settled down at a table near the buffet and were approached by a bunny waitress who cooed, "My name is Bunny. May I see your Playboy Club membership card, please?"

Richard reached first into one pocket then another and, frantically, another then looked at me and shouted, "You have it!"

"No, I don't," I replied. "You picked it up at the entrance."

Dick scrambled through his pockets again, stood up and made another scene. To quiet him down, Miss Bunny went back to the entrance, explained the situation and, fortunately because of his previous tirade, he was remembered and a duplicate card was issued immediately.

It was then that I realized my former neighbor, 'Hots' Michaels, was at the piano. I went up, shook hands, and we exchanged small talk. I was really embarrassed. But that was only the beginning.

The Playboy Clubs were designed on three levels with different entertainment on each. After raiding the food on the First Floor buffet, Richard took over my plate and suggested I go for another. It was then that he started "collecting" some of the Playboy promotional items on the table...silverware, ashtray, vase. Thank God, no one noticed, or if they did, said nothing.

After a couple of screwdrivers (vodka and orange juice which Minns claimed was a health drink), we took the elevator to the second floor. More goodies for the pocket and one that didn't fit...a genuine Playboy Club lamp. We didn't stay there long. Then we took the elevator to the third floor...with the lamp...where we were greeted by a bouncer when the door opened. He had heard about Richard from the previous floor guards and was ready for him.

First, he requested he return the lamp. Minns argued that he owned these fabulous health clubs and wanted to open a Playboy Club in Houston and needed the items as samples of what to order when he opened his own Playboy. The guard was understanding, thanked Dick for the lamp, which he took out of his hand, and suggested that he get a Playboy merchandise catalog and order what he needed.

Then, the final blow. On that third level, a charming young singer was belting her heart out when Richard decided to make it a duet letting me know that he really had a very good voice. After a few bars, evidently nobody else agreed and we were escorted to the elevator, down to the first floor and out the front door. Whatta memory!

Planning advertising and publicity for the Ace Rican club was always a hassle. Account executive Joanne Kopecky, who drove a gorgeous red convertible that I coveted, went through hell with Dick practically every day on how and what the ads should say. She felt they were misleading...actually, dishonest. They were.

One time, I was assigned the task of locating free *before* and *after* models to pose for the Ace Rican ads with less than a day to do it. Naturally, no one wanted to pose for free, so he hit on the idea of staging the shot using someone I knew for *before* and me for *after.*

Dick reluctantly gave me a $10 budget for the heavyweight which wound up being Ann Criswell, food editor of the Houston Chronicle at the time. She wasn't really that heavy, but it worked. We both wore black leotards and tights and posed in the exact same position, holding onto a bookcase, sidewise. I squirmed while the photographer strained to get just the right shot. Now you know how "before" and "afters" are made.

Always looking ahead, Richard wanted to take Ace Rican a step higher. He began plans for a posh executive type venture which he initially named The President's Health Club (eventually President/First Lady) to occupy the near downtown Houston Central National Bank building's lobby level. Glenn McCarthy's Cork Club had already moved from the Shamrock to the penthouse. McCarthy and Minns were good friends and they often lunched at the President's Health Club which served light health food. Also, many of the Cork Club patrons who had imbibed a little too much, came down for the oxygen fix the Club offered. It was a chummy relationship. Business tycoon Kenneth Schnitzer owned the building and we opened many of his other Houston projects. Just one big happy family!

Dr. Bob Delmontique was Richard's "star" partner in the venture which eventually spread across the nation. Anything but shy about his physical attributes, Delmontique was a part owner/operator of Executive Health Clubs International which currently operates 500 facilities worldwide with over five million members.

As a renowned fitness consultant and bodybuilder, Dr. Delmontique claimed to have worked with John Wayne, Errol Flynn, Marilyn Monroe, Clark Gable, astronaut John Glenn and, more recently, Matt Dillon. In his mid-80s Delmontique still runs marathons and bench presses over 250 pounds, probably a world record for his age. He still looks great!

My job then was to promote Dr. Delmontique as the world's most amazing health and fitness guru. He certainly looked the part. At that time, he claimed to be fifty with the body of a twenty year old which made a good news story once or twice...but not forever. Richard, who worked out obsessively, himself, at the Club and regularly celebrated his birthday with a twenty-four hour water skiing marathon on Lake Tahoe, was in awe of Delmontique and aspired to look like him. That was difficult because Richard was probably around 5' 9" and Delmontique was well over six feet. A handsome hulk of a man with bulging biceps.

The President's Health Club opening was spectacular. Lots of food, champagne and music and only one guest fell into the pool. It was an instant success. The press loved it.

Client presentations at the Richard L. Minns Agency were show stoppers. We had scripts, rehearsals, music, the works. We rehearsed at our regular Monday morning meetings when Richard would rant, rave, insult and inspire his stable of employees to accomplish bigger and better things... if they wanted to remain employed.

Would-be clients were overwhelmed by the magnitude of a Minns presentation. Especially when Dick would grin, look over at me, and ask, "Do you think we should put news about (client) in Time, Life and Fortune all in the same week or should we spread it out over a month?" Whatta joke!

Dick and Mimi Minns were, like many of my other employers, total opposites. She, quiet but forceful when it came to the bookkeeping. He was loud and overbearing. But they both seemed to agree on two things –making money and a lavish lifestyle – brash and gaudy. They had the first super sized round revolving bed with a bright red spread on a pedestal in their bedroom with an exposed bathtub at one side.

No gathering at the Minns abode was ever complete without crab claws, a sign of prosperity, Richard claimed. That included the annual staff Christmas party they threw at their home. We still use the set of steak knives he gave me over forty years ago.

Another client was Abe Krell. He created Rootox and Ridex, both biodegradable drain protecting products that are still on the market. Another interesting client was Spare Tire, an injection liquid that repaired flat tires. Just spray it in the damaged tire, and, hopefully, it would be good as new in minutes. Or so they claimed.

We did a television show for Carnation Milk. To attract children, I was instructed to find a character they couldn't resist. I wound up with a little old lady by the name of Mother Goose. Dressed in her long country costume complete with bonnet and a fake goose in her basket, she told stories to children at birthday parties. It was decided to use her on the Carnation Milk television show.

I contacted her by phone and she agreed to stop by the agency for an interview. By this time we were located in Minns new digs...a fairly large building on trendy Montrose in Houston named, naturally, the Richard L. Minns building. On the day Mother Goose was to arrive, we got a call. "This is the Yellow Cab driver. I gotta lady here who says she's Mother Goose and don't know where she's going. Can you help her?"

We directed him to the agency and in no time, Mother Goose arrived. Needless to say, she gave the agency staff a laugh, but she was a real hit on TV. The kids loved her.

The last Minns agency presentation I made was for Del Webb and a new project scheduled for an area around League City, to be known as Clear Lake City. We had handled publicity and advertising for Webb's first Sun City, retirement center in Phoenix, Arizona and were gearing up to promote this new development.

Dominated by rice paddies and scrub brush, the multi-acre site was to simulate a complete city with all of the amenities including business, retail, recreational and residential. Actually, it was planned before NASA headquarters was announced for the same area. The connection would become an unbeatable sales tool attracting astronauts and support industry executives to buy the homes and partake in the recreational amenities.

We turned in our presentation, no dog and pony show this time. We were notified by Webb that although we had the winning plan, he would have to bow to his partner's (Humble Oil) selection...Weekley & Valenti. Both Weldon Weekley and Jack Valenti had worked for Humble Oil before it became Exxon. They opened their agency based on their recommendations and their ordering premium items for Conoco gas station giveaways.

By this time, Richard Minns was more deeply involved in health clubs (which I hated) allowing his more diversified client base to fall by the wayside. He suggested that since I had made the winning presentation to Del Webb for Clear Lake City, I should discuss being a part of the Weekley & Valenti Agency.

I didn't see or hear from Dick Minns for quite a few years after I had opened my own pr agency. One day in 1980 he called to invite me to a political fundraiser at his new home. I think he and Mimi had separated. They had three children, all with names beginning with "M' – Mitzi, Matthew, and Mike, now a prominent Houston advocacy attorney. Minns also said he wanted to talk to me about helping to promote his new health club venture,The Olympia, which he said would be the epitome of health clubs in the world.

I accepted his invitation and went to his lavish home where I was shocked. He still had that little boy grin with a fantastic muscular body, but he had colored his hair bright orange. (I think he wanted it to be blond but ran into a color pigment problem). It was a real eye catcher.

It was also a surprise to find him connected to politics. Unlike Sylvan Brown and Jack Valenti, Richard Minns had showed no signs of political connections when I worked for him. This was a new Richard L. Minns.

He introduced me to his partner for his new venture -- Melvin Lane Powers. A huge gorilla-like man, he nodded hello and I gasped. I had heard and read about Powers in the past. His aunt was Candice Mossler, a bubbly blond socialite married to a wealthy older man, Jacques Mossler.

In 1961, at 6-foot-4 and just 20 years old (who could pass for 35) Melvin Lane Powers, the son of Candice Mossler's older sister, came to live with her and Jacques and their collective six children. Powers had just served a short jail sentence for being part of a swindle racket. The hope was that he would reform under the influence of wealth and social contact. Jacques Mossler gave Powers a job and, reportedly, was grooming him to take over his business. It was also reputed that Candice took Powers on, too... as a lover.

Three years later (1964) millionaire banker Jacques Mossler, age 69, was found bludgeoned and stabbed to death in his Florida apartment, presumably by an unknown assailant. However, circumstantial evidence pointed to the related lovers. Further investigations brought an indictment of Candace, and the alleged killer, Melvin Lane Powers.

After eighteen months of legal maneuvering, the two went to trial: she with high-profile Houston defense attorneys Clyde Woody and Marian Rosen; Powers with the notorious Percy Foreman and William F. Walsh.

Prosecutors sought the death penalty, contending the two had plotted Mossler's murder to get his fortune and continue a "torrid and incestuous love affair."

According to a Houston Chronicle article by Stan Redding, an Arkansas convict called as a prosecution witness testified that Powers had offered him money to "do away with an old mooch". On the other side, a

Texas convict serving time for theft testified that Mrs. Mossler gave him a $7000 down payment in 1962 to kill her husband. Two months later, the pair was acquitted by a jury because it was surmised that the prosecution relied too heavily on criminals' testimony.

At the time, Powers was selling trailer homes in Webster, Texas where he claimed to be at the time of the murder. After acquittal, he went on to dabble in real estate and investments which brought him in contact with Richard L. Minns. I wondered what Minns was doing with a partner like Melvin Powers. He was always raunchy, but not criminal, I thought.

Our next meeting was at the Olympia which was being built at the top of a building in north Houston. We discussed a plan for the grand opening and I was introduced to Dick's new friend, a pretty young, blond woman...**Barbara Piotrowski.**

Barbara had met Minns at a ski lodge in Colorado. A pre-med student, she had been a California beauty queen and was recovering from a love affair that went wrong. She had never met anyone quite like Richard L. Minns, twenty-four years her junior, and was completely captivated by him. I think he mentioned that he was married, but was in the process of getting a divorce. Shortly thereafter, she came to Houston to join him, working as an aerobics instructor at the Olympia.

I met with her several times to get publicity information and photos to promote the Olympia's opening. Minns had set her up in a townhouse and kept her on a strict budget, sometimes not even a quarter for a cup of coffee, promising that when his divorce became final, all of that would change. And did it ever!

Once Dick's divorce from Mimi was finalized, he told Barbara they were through. Hurt and angry, she removed all of the contents from the townhouse and moved out. Minns was livid, charged her with theft and reported the incident to the police. He insisted everything in the home was his and was moved without his knowledge or permission. The feud went on for days, making front page news, until one afternoon in 1981 at around 5:30, Barbara Piotrowski was shot four times in front of a donut shop on Westheimer, one of Houston's busiest streets near the Galleria Mall.

Minns was immediately tagged as a suspect, but was never charged. He skipped town with some of his millions and became an itinerant millionaire seeking protection in Switzerland and other European countries.

It is believed that he ultimately settled in Canada where he remarried and started a second family.

Piotrowski survived the shooting but was paralyzed from the chest down and was confined to a wheel chair, vowing to walk again and to make Minns pay. After many court appearances, she was awarded, according to varying reports, from $30 to $60 million from her former lover which she has yet to collect.

To escape public scrutiny, Barbara changed her name to Janni Smith. In 1982, following her interest in medicine, she became an assistant to Nobel Prize candidate Dr. Jerold Petrovsky who was researching the feasibility of attaching computer controlled electrodes to paralyzed legs to enable them to function.

Demonstrating the system, Barbara walked again for the first time in 1985 and went on to compete in marathons and pursue her work with the handicapped. In1991, Barbara Piotrowski /Janni Smith became Mrs. Janni Petrovsky.

In 1992, her ordeal with Minns was portrayed in a television movie, *Sleeping with the Devil,* which provided the financial means of furthering her medical studies. Mrs. Petrovsky is still waiting for the dollar return from her suits against Minns and the Houston

Police Department, which she insists did not properly respond to her charges.

The actual shooters, Patrick Steen and Nathaniel Ivery, were charged with attempted murder and are serving 35 year sentences. Bob Anderson and private detective Dudley Bell were both convicted of solicitation of capital murder and each received thirty-eight year prison terms.

Minns, still on the lam, was confronted in Dallas a few years ago on suspicion of holding illegal passports but was released. He also made news in a suit his ex-wife Mimi filed for ownership of some existing health clubs.

Mimi Minns contacted me shortly after her divorce from Dick was final and asked me to review some paintings her new friend, a retired military man, had done. I met the couple at their gated townhouse and advised him to create more paintings to justify a gallery showing. The couple married and moved to Arkansas.

And Melvin Powers. I have always felt that he was behind all of this. Known for his bungling of shady deals and his criminal history, it seems he would have been a logical suspect for the murder solicitation. Especially since Richard L. Minns was always calculating and shrewd in his dealings. He would never have scheduled the tragedy for 5:30 in the afternoon in one of Houston's highest profile neighborhoods. I don't think so.

Where is Richard L. Minns today? While surfing the net in December of 2008 I found the official Richard L. Minns website and was dumbfounded. Dick Minns, the brash adman I had known for years is now a famed sculptor creating biblical and mythical figures in bronze in his studio in Hadassah Neurim overlooking the Mediterranean Sea.

According to his website, Minns was diagnosed with type T3 prostate cancer in 2003, which he overcame on a pill diet he devised on his own (typical Minns!) He claims, "Cancer made me the sculptor I am today."

In keeping with his tradition of breaking records, at 70, he waterskied the Kinneret (biblical Sea of Galilee) and repeated the feat two years later with his then 12 year old son Sean. At 79 (July 2008) he has five children, seven grandchildren and three great grandchildren and is renowned throughout Israel as a master sculptor combining creative talent with his personal background in bodybuilding and athletic achievement. Want to know more about the Dick Minns phenomena? http://www.minnsart.com

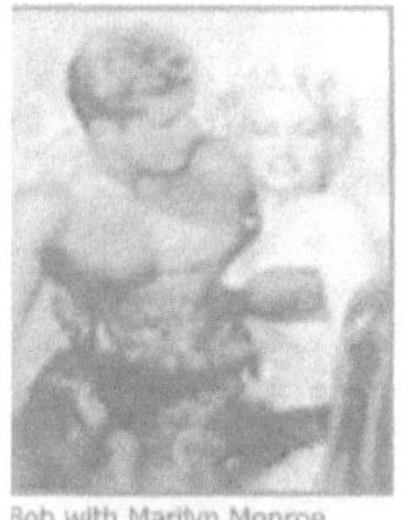

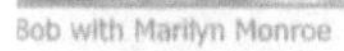

Bob Delmontique,
health club wonder.

Melvin Powers,
notorious entrepreneur.

Dick Minns with one of
his bronze sculptures.

Richard L. Minns, now sculpting
bigger than life.

CHAPTER 7

Jack Valenti – The Presidents' Choice

Jack Valenti, a prominent University of Houston alumnus with an MBA from Harvard, always had his sights set on greener political pastures. I never dreamed he would become one of my biggest star encounters, representing the industry of the stars as president of the Motion Picture Association of America.

My former husband had known Valenti and his sidekick, Councilman Johnny Goyen from the good old U of H days. So in the spring of 1961, I had sort of an *in* besides my Del Webb favored Clear Lake City presentation when I went to talk to Valenti about a job with his agency. It didn't take long. In a few days, I was vice president of public relations at Weekley & Valenti Advertising Agency.

One of Houston's youngest high school graduates at fifteen, Valenti went to work as an office boy for Humble Oil & Refining Company (now Exxon Mobil) going to the University of Houston at night. He worked his way up to a spot in the advertising department before leaving to join the U.S. Air Force (1942-45) as pilot and commander of B-25 bombers. He received the Distinguished Flying Cross and the Air Medal with three clusters for his 51 missions over Europe.

Upon discharge, Valenti returned to the Humble advertising department, headed by the charismatic Pop Mabry, where he met his future partner, Weldon Weekley. At the time, Jack had dramatically increased Humble's sales through a unique "clean bathroom" campaign he super minded. He was ready to succeed again.

In 1952, Weekley and Valenti decided to go after Continental Oil Company's sales promotion business and opened their own advertising agency with Humble's blessing. Like all of the other seemingly mismatched partners I had encountered, Jack and Weldon seemed the perfect opposites. Valenti was the small talkative social one who always had a smile and a handshake upfront. Weekley was a big man, shy and sometimes clumsy in social situations. He was also a male chauvinist. I remember how surprised he was that after I left his agency I opened my own. As Rosalie, his wife, put it when they ran into me at a Heritage Society open house, "What did you think she was going to do? Stay home and knit."

Valenti had been exposed to politics early in life. Second generation Italians, his family played an important role in early Houston elections representing their Italian/ Greek neighborhood in sought after votes by local politicians. His father was a clerk in the Harris County Courthouse and Jack learned early that an extended hand and a smile to the right people could accomplish great things. Valenti actually started campaigning and schmoozing at age ten and excelled in high school debate which prepared him for his future public speaking successes.

Politicians were immediately drawn to Jack. His smooth, easy-going manner and knack of saying "nothing" in hundreds of eloquent well chosen words, was recognized and admired by political leaders throughout the state, especially by his closest friend and admirer, late Houston Councilman Johnny Goyen who seemed to be his shadow.

Lyndon Johnson was the Senate majority leader when he met Jack. Impressed by his energy and winning ways, he awarded him the publicity consulting contract for the presidential campaign in 1961. The relationship flowered with Valenti's many visits to Washington DC, which also included bonding with

Johnson's executive secretary, Mary Margaret Wiley. He later wooed and married her. The couple had three children, Courtenay, John and Alexandra.

I saw then Vice President and Lady Bird often since I worked on the promotion of their Austin, Texas media holdings: a newspaper, radio station and a television station. Many times over lunch at the Houston Club, I talked with Lady Bird about life in the White House while Jack and Lyndon discussed other business and politics.

Vice President Johnson was always cordial, but nothing like the late Lady Bird. She was warm and wonderful. I recall complimenting her on a dress she was wearing. "Yes," she smiled, "I liked it so much I bought it on sale in several different colors." She was a REAL person and she is sorely missed.

I saw her a few times after that and was really sad when she passed away (July, 2007). She was truly a great lady who contributed so much to the environment and to the beauty of Texas and the world.

Getting started on the Clear Lake City project, formally announced in January of 1962, was a real challenge since it involved so many facets: retail, commercial, hotels, restaurants, recreation, single and multi-family housing.

Located off State Highway 3, a mile west of Clear Lake in southeast Harris County, Clear Lake City would also became the home of choice for many of the first astronauts and support industry executives. Ultimately, it become a tourist destination because of its proximity to the NASA space Center, Galveston and nearby fishing and boating centers.

In 1963, Vice President Johnson asked Valenti to handle the publicity and press relations for a political tour. **President John F. Kennedy** was planning to beef up Texas' support. Stops were scheduled in Ft. Worth, Austin, Dallas and Houston. Jack, who always called me *ReetZ* (Rita Zenzen combo) asked me to produce the programs and handle publicity and press relations for the events.

The program format was purposely kept simple so that it could easily be adapted to each of the four stops to reduce printing costs. The only difference would be Houston where President Kennedy would be attending a dinner honoring Congressman Albert Thomas who was seeking re-election and looking for more support.

Front cover of the program pictured the Texas state capitol in an oval with the words "Texas welcomes the President of the United States and the Vice President of the United States". Inside the one I managed to save was the program for the Austin dinner scheduled for November 22, which like the Dallas lunch planned for that afternoon, never happened.

Late afternoon on November 21, 1963, I brought the proofs of the program to the Rice Hotel for Johnson and Kennedy to approve. Security was really heavy and I didn't have a pass, so I walked briskly through the halls to Vice President Johnson's suite smiling, waving hello and looking like I knew where I was going. Nobody stopped me.

The Vice President recognized me from before and knew I was representing Jack Valenti. He took the copy, personally, to President Kennedy and in minutes returned with it approved. The Albert Thomas program was already at the dinner so I took the proofs of the remaining programs back to the printer with the okay to run them off and ship them overnight. I then hurried to attend the Albert Thomas event myself.

Next day Ed Tron, who worked on the Clear Lake City advertising account, and I were driving down highway

59 toward Clear Lake City listening to the radio when an announcer broke into the music... "President John F. Kennedy has been shot". We looked at each other stunned, tears swelling up in our eyes. It was unbelievable. But we had a job to do. So we pulled ourselves together and proceeded on to Clear Lake City.

Valenti had made the trip to Dallas on Air Force One with the Kennedys, Johnsons and John Connallys. In the motorcade at the time of the tragedy, Valenti was riding ten cars behind the President's vehicle which included the First Lady, the Johnsons and the Connallys. Within hours after President Kennedy's death, Valenti was on Air Force One again. This time witnessing Johnson being sworn in as president. Jack Valenti was then appointed special assistant to President Lyndon B. Johnson. He never returned to work at the agency.

Texas Governor John B. Connally, whose campaign Jack had worked on, formally opened Clear Lake City on January 15, 1963. Although construction had dragged, Del Webb was adamant that the project open as originally scheduled. For publicity starters, he invited *star* friends to visit, eat at the unfinished Country Club and inspect the unfinished luxury homes, recreation center and Kings Inn Hotel.

The first such celebrity was **Jimmy Stewart** and his wife, Gloria. We had lunch at the Clear Lake Country Club overlooking the golf course and had cocktails in one of the luxury, almost finished, homes. How amazing to be sitting and chatting casually with THE Jimmy Stewart. Tall, gangly, slow talking, and o-so-charming. It was almost better than a Hy-Shopper interview.

Although Jack was gone, the agency continued to get other politically related accounts like Continental Airlines, Anheuser Busch, the Shell Dredgers vs the Oyster Fishermen and the Port Cotton Warehouses vs Interior Warehousing owners which required me to travel to political hearings across the country and keep the media on our side. I remember a trip to Miami with Weldon Weekley.

We had to sit in on a series of hearings regarding cotton being held up at the port rather than being shipped out, thus affecting work schedules of the Longshoremen's Union members. They were represented at the hearings by a surly, burly loud bunch of irate laborers.

After a hearing, I went back to my hotel room and double-locked the door. I was really a little scared. The only disturbance was a knock on the door...from

Weldon Weekley. I wondered what he wanted at that time of night. Guess I'll never know; I just told him to go away.

In 1965, Anheuser-Busch announced that it would build a new brewery in Houston. A national favorite beer, Budweiser was not tops in Texas. The brewery had lost many friends several years before when a refrigerated rail car with Budweiser headed for Texas broke down, causing the beer to go sour and have an unpleasant taste. With the new brewery Anheuser-Busch hoped to overcome their bad reputation and gain flavor favor among the Lone Star State's big beer drinkers.

Even though he was no longer active with the agency, it was probably Jack's political connections that got Weekley and Valenti the Anheuser Busch public relations account for its new brewery. I was assigned to handle the job. Not only was it a great public relations opportunity for me, I also got to network with some of best agencies in the country who represented A/B.

Meeting the original **August Busch**, for the first time was a thrilling experience.. He was a rather short bubbly energetic man who took pride in his product and in his hometown of St. Louis, Missouri. While at an ad agency brain storming session in St. Louis, Busch took me and a group of other agency reps on a tour of *his* city. It was awesome.

Deciding on a theme for the Houston brewery opening was a no brainer. They wanted to fit into the Old West, so that's what we did. With the help of Breede decorators, an authentic old western town was constructed on the vacant brewery site to whet the appetites of media and the public.

The grand opening was a huge success and resulted in unbelievable publicity and city-wide good will. Hit of the event was the appearance of the internationally famous Clydesdale horses. They were housed at the Post Oak stables, not too far from the old Channel 2 television studios where they were scheduled to appear live on an afternoon talk show. There was no easy way to get them there, so we decided to walk them the approximate three mile distance.

We thought we had allowed plenty of time, but traffic was extra heavy and it took much longer than expected. We arrived at the station just in time for host Chris Chandler to announce, "Here they come...they're coming down the street right now. They're almost here..." But we never did get there for the planned interview. So much work for so little reward.

In addition to turning out continuing publicity on the progress of brewery construction, beer recipes and all good things about Anheuser-Busch, I was asked to design the brewery's information tour. The norm for A/B breweries was to have visitors walk through the tour to learn how the beer was made, and then on to the hospitality room where free beer samples were available. Which is why visitors came in the first place.

On a trip to Florida to study the Busch gardens there, I was amazed at the numbers of retirees in line who commented, "Didn't have anything to do today so decided to get some free beer. It's worth taking the tour again."

I also had to work with the designer of a giant animated neon eagle sign, A/B's signature logo, which Busch wanted mounted on the front of the building. Actually, the thing was jinxed from the beginning. It flapped its wings, via neon, unevenly, intermittently and sometimes, not at all. It was a disaster.

Fortunately, during a recent plant remodeling which increased capacity from the initial one million barrels of beer a year to 20 million barrels (one barrel contains 31 gallons) the emblem was removed. Or perhaps it had been gone a lot longer, since I didn't go back to check. A simple Budweiser logo is now blasted across the front of the brewery. Can't believe that in 2006-Busch celebrated its fortieth birthday in Houston.

One wonderful thing about August, Sr., he loved giveaways. Well, maybe not *give,* but brewery memorabilia like imitation pewter mugs, lovelier watches, evening bags, branding irons and much more... all with his beloved flying eagle emblem prominently displayed. I have a collection of most of the items which I still treasure. All of them were sold at the brewery gift shops.

Mr. Busch also loved big parties. There were annual distributor gatherings in exciting places. I attended the one in Los Angeles, California, staying at the Beverly Wilshire Hotel where I spied many stars including **Lee Marvin** sitting at the hotel bar. The A/B event was held at the Hilton Hotel and entertainment was top drawer – **Frank Sinatra**. I never had it that good before. Nothing like the Richard L. Minns traveling days.

About this time the nation's first covered sports arena, the Houston Astrodome, was opened and Anheuser-Busch was one of the first to sign up for a VIP skybox. It was an ideal place to create good will with the media and clients. A/B was very generous in allowing me to use it so that the local brewery executives could meet the press.

Already the owner of several Busch Gardens and theme parks across the country, A/B wanted to open one as a part of the Houston brewery. Land was available and they felt it would do well. I researched the project and because of its then rather remote location and the opening of Astroworld not too far away, I recommended that they junk the idea. But they didn't.

Long after I left Weekley and Valenti, Houston Busch Gardens opened. About two years later, it closed and was totally demolished to provide land for a brewery expansion. I told them so.

Weldon Weekley had volunteered me to create a special event for the Texas Society of Professional Engineers to draw public attention to how engineers benefit the community. At the time, there was great controversy over the health hazards of Buffalo Bayou which wove its way through downtown Houston. Long considered a giant sewer holding all of the wastes from downtown Houston, the engineers noted that with the completion of the Lockwood Sewage Treatment Plant, all wastes would be diverted out of the bayou and through that plant.

Recalling my time in Europe, I remembered the Paris sewer tours which were and still are conducted. I worked with the Houston city staff and TSPE reps to devise a plan for a Houston Sewer Tour. It happened in about 1966. The sewer cover was opened in front of the old Post Office on San Jacinto street and some little carts were lined up to tour visitors under the city and follow the waste flow from downtown to the Lockwood plant. It created lots of public interest and was featured in the newspapers, radio and television news. It was Houston's first and last Sewer Tour.

Continental Airlines wanted to expand its overseas connections and came to Weekley & Valenti for help to promote a partnership with Pan American Airways on a flight emanating from Houston and ending in Hawaii. Working with Continental's representative Bill Barron, I was flown to California to observe their hostess training school and gather material for publicity and feature stories to promote the inaugural flight and encourage future travel from Houston to Hawaii.

The ultimate plan had to be showy and attract area wide interest in the new connection to the islands.

Having worked with Foley's Department Store in downtown Houston on several successful promotions, I convinced Dorothy Young, special events coordinator at the time, to have Foley's sponsor the promotion focusing on travel to Hawaii in most of their departments including travel office, luggage, clothing and home decor...all aimed at Hawaii with appropriate decorations and special events.

The store would include Continental and Pan Am logos in their advertising, store windows and in-store displays. We designed special events with personal appearances of Hawaiian guests at the store and at radio, television and print interviews. I had fabric designed with the airlines' logos and had it made into Hawaiian shirts so that the guests could be immediately identified with Continental and Pan American.

The airlines invited Young and me to fly to Hawaii to "get in the mood" and meet some of the celebrities who could be a part of the promotion. We decided on **Duke Kahanamoku**, a Hawaiian legend known as the father of surfing and two members of his Duke's Surfing Team, Fred Hemmings and Paul Strauch. We visited with Don Ho at his Honolulu night club but he had conflicting engagements and could not participate.

The trio arrived, by Continental Airlines of course, and were taken to their hotel where they were given their schedules...and their promotional Hawaiian shirts. The Duke, who was a truly kind, wonderful amazing man, wore his faithfully at every public event and media interview. He brought me a wood sculpture of a Hawaiian god I still cherish and think of him every time I look at it.

We were lucky to have the Duke because in 1968, just a couple of years later, he passed away. Recognized worldwide as the father of modern surfing which in 1821 had been outlawed as immoral by European missionaries, Duke Kahanamoku revived the *sport of kings* with a board he crafted from a local sugar pine which he introduced in 1914 at Freshwater Beach, Australia. He took a young woman for a tandem ride making her that country's first surfer.

Paoa (Duke in Hawaiian) Kahanamoku received his father's name in honor of the Duke of Edinburgh who visited the island just before has father's birth in 1840. Years of surfing and rough water swimming made The Duke a great athlete and he traveled the country demonstrating his new style of surf boarding and gaining status as a world class swimmer. Duke

Kahanamoka took the Olympic gold medal in 1912. Eight years later, at age 30, he took the silver. He served as honorary sheriff of Honolulu, appeared in several Hollywood films and became Hawaii's official greeter.

Fred Hemmings, now often seen on television as a surfer competition commentator, and **Paul Strauch**, best known for his "Paul Strauch Five" or "Cheater Five" surfing maneuver, were among the chosen few to be included in the Duke Kahanamoku Surfer Team formed in 1965. Created by Kimo McVay, the Duke's manager, the team was organized to promote surfing and Duke surfing products, which made them naturals for the Continental- Pan Am/Foley's Houston promotion.

Hemmings and Strauch were both surfing champions from 1958 to 1969. Hemmings was the founder/producer of the Triple Crown of Surfing from 1982 to 1989, is an accomplished outrigger canoe racer and an international marathon runner. He has been a national television commentator on surfing and canoe racing on ABC Wide World of Sports, CBS Sports Spectacular and NBC Sports World. A recovered polio victim, Fred Hemmings was inducted into the International Surfing Hall of Fame in 1991 and the

Hawaii State Sports Hall of Fame in 1998. As a member of the Hawaii state legislature in the 1980s, he gained a reputation as an effective and vigorous leader with expertise as a political economist. Hemmings has authored three books including *The Soul of Surfing in Hawaii.*

In the mid-60s, Fred and Paul were handsome, muscular and polite young men who made a hit wherever they appeared. Not quite so cooperative when it came to wearing the promotion shirts, however; they would always apologize that they had forgotten them. But no one was required to wear promo shirts when we went to dinner at the Shamrock Hotel's Emerald Room to see the **Dinah Shore** show.

After Dinah finished her show, she sent a waiter with a note. She would like to meet Duke Kahanamoku in her suite to discuss surfing lessons for her daughter on their upcoming trip to Hawaii. We went up to see her and the Duke told her he would make all of the arrangements and looked forward to seeing them in Hawaii.

One of the advantages of being associated with a politically popular advertising agency with national accounts is recognition and appointments to classy groups like the San Antonio Hemisfair committee for the 1968 World's Fair in San Antonio which brought me regularly to that city and got me VIP treatment while visiting the international event.

Built in a downtown park bordering a decaying neighborhood known as Lavaca, Hemisfair transposed San Antonio from a laid back military town with a large Mexican population to a world class tourist and commercial destination. We now live in the recently revived Lavaca neighborhood which is a recognized historic district just in back of Hemisfair park and the 600+ foot Tower of the Americas.

Long after Jack Valenti left his agency, Weldon Weekley got a new partner...Ed Penney, a complete Valenti opposite. No imagination, no fun, no personality. And, I guess the feeling was mutual. I had too much energy for him. Whatever the reason, Weldon Weekley called me into his office one Friday afternoon and announced that I would no longer be a part of Weekley and Penney as of the following Monday. I was in the middle of a big press promotion for Anheuser Busch and a special event in their sky box. I asked what I had done and why wasn't I given any notice.

I had never been fired before and didn't know how to react. I went back to my office to think about it and returned to Weldon's office telling him that it would be only fair to have a two-week notice so that I could wind up projects in motion and disappear gracefully. He said that was impossible because people were always fired on Friday and didn't return on Monday...and all of the staff was already aware of it. He also offered to pay me my regular salary for six months if I didn't tell anyone that I was fired. Didn't know what I would tell anyone, but the money came in handy.

However, I got the last "laugh". The following Monday, I did return to my office and went about business as usual. Naturally, the staff was in shock. But, Weldon wouldn't stand for it. I was crushed. Where next?

Weldon and wife Rosalie Weekley will be forever remembered for the new Southwest Houston YMCA that was renamed The Weekley Family YMCA. In 2001, sons Richard, Robert and David, donated a million dollars to honor their parents with the facility that replaced the Y that they had attended as children. My happy memory of the Weekleys is a hand beaded cashmere cardigan they brought back from a Hong Kong trip for me. It's almost an antique now.

In November of 1966, Jack Valenti's Houston friends threw an appreciation dinner for him. Prominent attorney Leon Jaworski of Fullbright, Crooker, Freeman, Bates & Jaworski was general chairman and master of ceremonies. Many of Jack's old buddies, led by Councilman Johnny Goyen, were on hand to meet and greet him.

Valenti left President Johnson and his Washington advisory post to take over the reins of the Motion Picture Association of America (MPAA) where he distinguished himself as one of the most active, productive lobbyists ever. He remolded the movie rating system and became a Hollywood icon admired around the world. He was among the highest paid Washington trade organization executives with an annual salary of about $1.35 million.

Valenti was a prolific writer of everything: speeches, newspaper and magazine articles and four books. His 1992 political novel, *Protect and Defend*, was edited by former first lady Jacqueline Kennedy. Valenti retired from MPAA in 2004 and in 2006 he wrote his memoirs,

This Time, This Place: My Life in War, the White House and Hollywood.

Jack Joseph Valenti died from complications of a stroke on April 26, 2007.

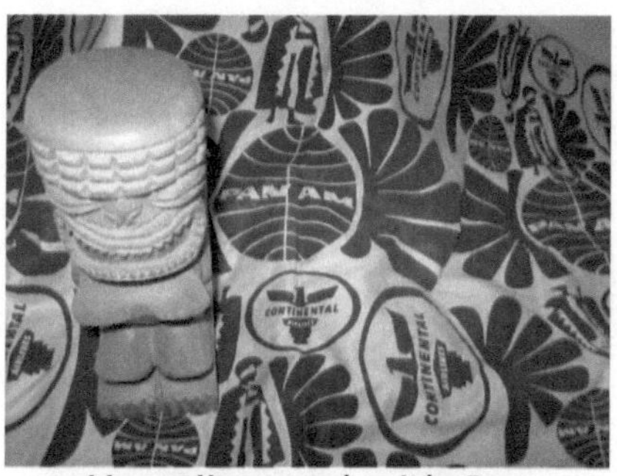

Hawaiian god with Pan American-Continental promotional fabric.

Continental Airlines' Bill Barron and wife share a table with Duke Kahanamoku and me at the Shamrock.

Introducing Hawaiian surfers Paul Strauch and Fred Hemmings to KXYZ's Fred "Mr. Hollywood" Nahas at the Shamrock.

The Duke's Surf Team: Paul Strauch, left, Fred Hemmings, right.

PROGRAM

Entrance of Guests to Head Tables, 7:30 p.m.

INVOCATION
Dr. Robert Tate
Minister of the First Methodist Church, Austin

NATIONAL ANTHEM

Introduction of Members of the Texas House of Representatives
Byron Tunnell, Speaker of the House

Introduction of Members of the Texas Senate
Preston Smith, Lt. Governor of Texas

Introduction of Guests at Head Tables
Eugene Locke, Chairman State Democratic Executive Committee

Entrance of the Governor and Mrs. John Connally

Entrance of the Vice-President and Mrs. Lyndon B. Johnson

Entrance of the President and Mrs. John F. Kennedy

Welcome by Governor John Connally

Remarks by Vice-President Lyndon B. Johnson

Address by President John F. Kennedy

BENEDICTION
Very Reverend Edward C. Matocha
Chancellor of the Diocese of Austin

On the program: Texas welcomes Kennedy and Johnson.

Rear view: Valenti and Johnson

In a huddle:President Johnson, Jack Valenti, Hubert Humphries

Bomber pilot Jack Valenti won the Distinguished Flying Cross and the Air Medal of Honer with three clusters.

CHAPTER 8

On My Own

Sylvan Brown in Houston, like Al Dvorin in Chicago, was always an option when I needed a temporary professional home. He now had a few accounts that I could work with and one that was coming up. This time, he introduced me to his friend, **Sidney Schlenker** who with Allen Becker owned PACE Management, an entertainment management business.

Schlenker came from a wealthy Houston banking family and was an aggressive hustler. His partner, Allan Becker, was completely the opposite: quiet, shy and unassuming. PACE Management oversaw a kaleidescope of events from staged musical productions to demolition derbies to theme parks and sports events including the Houston Music Theater and later, Houston's Astroworld theme park (closed since 2002).

After several meetings with Sylvan and me, S. L. Brown & Associates was retained to handle publicity for the new Houston Music Theater-in-the-round.

Schlenker left PACE in 1966 to take charge of the Astrodome's marketing and sales. He was named chief executive officer and president of the Astrodomain Corporation and the Houston Astros Baseball team in 1975, after original owner Judge Roy Hofheinz suffered a stroke. He retained 45% ownership of PACE until the early 90s.

The aggressive entrepreneur then went on to successfully open and manage several projects across the country. One of his high profile ventures, the Memphis pyramid-shaped arena, failed in 1991 for lack of financing.

In 1995, Schlenker became involved with another biggie...the federal prosecution of Hollywood madam Heidi Fleiss. With actor Charlie Sheen and Mexican businessman Manuel Santos he was called to testify under a grant of limited immunity that they had written checks which were produced in court by three of Madam Fleiss' prostitutes to prove that she had laundered ill-gotten gains.

Sidney Shlenker suffered a spinal cord injury in a 1998 highway accident which rendered him a paraplegic. He died of heart failure in 2003 at age 66. It seems many of my friends should have stayed out of cars. He is survived by his wife Denise and children Joshua, Alana and Zachary. When I knew him, he had just divorced his first wife, Marty, who opened a trendy restaurant in Houston.

Allen Becker and his family continued to run PACE Entertainment, which became the world's largest privately owned concert, theater and promotions company, until 1998 when he sold it to SFX for $130 million. He currently manages Becker Interests, L.P. and the Becker Family Foundation with his wife, Shirley and children Gary, Brian and Sunni.

The Becker Foundation supports numerous civic, cultural, religious and medical causes. Becker was inducted into the Texas Business Hall of Fame in 2003 and received the Bernard B. Jakobs Award for Excellence in the American Theater in 2004. Just goes to show that those quiet ones can still make some noise.

After a few months back with S.L. Brown, we agreed that I should open my own agency. R. Z. Estes, Inc., my "old" name. I was divorced in mid-1967, the same year that the business opened. Sylvan gave me his blessing and the Houston Music Theater as my first account.

Brown was in the process of switching from creating ADDY (local) and CLEO (national) award-winning television commercials to concentrate on his exclusive computerized time scheduling system for radio and television which proved a great asset for time buyers and an instant money-maker for S. L. Brown. The transition gave him more time for his second passion, golf. Sylvan Brown died in 2002.

One of the first musicals at Houston Music Theater was *On A Clear Day,* starring **Van Johnson** and **Linda Lavin** (later star of "Alice" television series and many movies). Lavin was a young singer who had appeared with Johnson before and he looked after her like an older brother. After the show closed, Lavin stayed with us for a couple of weeks and took a side trip to Mexico, bringing back a pearl shell fish bottle opener which I still have.

I was back in my element – STARS! I was so excited to meet Van Johnson and went to rehearsal the night before opening to give him his schedule for television, radio and newspaper interviews. I kept motioning to him between scenes and finally he shouted out that he was rehearsing and did not want to be disturbed. I left.

A few hours later, the phone rang. "This is Van Johnson. I want to apologize for my bad behavior. I was just pre-occupied with the script and being in the *round,* something new for me. I just wasn't thinking ahead. Of course, I'll be happy to do any interviews you have lined up."

I couldn't believe it. Van Johnson who I had watched and loved in so many movies calling me to apologize and agreeing to do all of the interviews. I told him I would pick him up at his hotel at 9 the next morning. He immediately became my all-time favorite star.

We went on interviews practically every day of opening week stopping for lunch at the Warwick Club in between. We became friends. He told me he had just been hypnotized to stop smoking and was a little edgy. He also explained why he always wore red socks on stage... "For luck," he grinned.

There were no interviews scheduled for the second week of *On A Clear Day*. That first Monday, Van called and wondered where I was. I told him his publicity duties were over and I thought he would appreciate not being escorted around. Instead, he said he missed me and could we have lunch without interviews. I was thrilled and we did.

The Clear Day cast which included local talent **Georgia Creighton** was so warm and wonderful that I wanted to have a party for them at my house. I gave all of the cast a verbal invitation, but did not think that Van would be interested. He was such a celebrity and probably had so many other things to do. But he heard about the party and asked why I had not invited him. I explained and, sure enough, he arrived on party night with his good friend socialite Elly Fondren and a huge gift fruit basket.

Houston Post artist **Hap Garman** always did a caricature drawing of the current show cast, sitting in the audience during rehearsals in order to get it to the paper in time for the morning-after-opening reviews. He knew how much I liked Van and the cast of *Clear Day* and gave me the original drawing which hangs over our bed today.

Hap was a jolly little man who was a full time window trimmer at Foley's downtown Houston store. One of our favorite things was to get a brown bag lunch and eat in the window he was working on. He also did a great caricature of the Foley's downtown Christmas parade which I still have. He's been gone a long time, but I'll always remember him.

Tommy Tune was the tallest human I had ever seen. I was not aware of his awesome dancing ability. In 1966, when he returned to Houston from New. York.

It was the first summer that the Houston Music theater was open and he assisted the choreographer in staging some numbers. Tune had been assistant choreographer for The Dean Martin television show. He received his MA in theater arts from the University of Houston and had gone to New York to seek his fortune. Tune was fun to have around; always playing jokes on the other cast members.

Tommy Tune went on to appear in movies (Ambrose in Hello Dolly), on Broadway and television. He has won nine Tony Awards, more than any other performer, was inducted into the Theatre Hall of Fame and has his own star on the Hollywood Walk of Fame. He renewed his dancing acquaintance with Sandy Duncan, initiated in Houston when she was 12 and he was 19, in Broadway productions *Two for the Show* and *My One and Only.* He's a Houston icon!

Patrice Munsel, her husband and their four children were featured in *The Sound of Music* at the theater. For fun, I took them all to Westbury Square, a quaint early American themed retail center in southwest Houston popular in the 60's. We had ice cream at Rumplemeyer's old fashioned ice cream parlor. It was a great place. Sad to say the entire center disappeared as

Houston reinforced its image of teardown old and rebuild new. I brought my daughters Vikii and Lori to see Sound of Music on opening night and Munsel posed for a picture with them. They loved it.

Canadian vocalist **Gisele MacKenzie** played Mamma Rose in *Gypsy* at the Houston Music Theater. She had appeared in early television shows including *The Jack Benny Program, Ed Sullivan* and was later featured on *Your Hit Parade.*

MacKenzie had two small children who were traveling with her. Since she was having an affair with the show's director who traveled with them, she wanted some privacy so I volunteered to keep them at my home for a couple of days since I had a live-in housekeeper. She was most grateful and the kids were much fun.

Gypsy was a happy musical with lots of pretty girls which I brought to entertain at a Houston Chamber of Commerce luncheon. **Larry Marcus,** manager of Nieman Marcus-downtown Houston, and **Bobby Sakowitz**, downtown Sakowitz owner/manager, were both swingers when it came to the ladies. At the *Gypsy* lunch, they vied for the attention of the sexy starlets much like teenagers. They both followed them to the elevator attempting to make a date. Their downtown stores have long since disappeared from the Houston scene, but the magic they brought in those days will never be forgotten.

Sakowitz's sister, Lynn, was married to sometimes shady oil tycoon Oscar Wyatt who more recently was called on the carpet for his overseas shenanagans.

Georgia Creighton, who had gone to New York to find success, wanted to stay in her Houston hometown for a while after *On A Clear Day so s*he took on the role of Tessie Turra, one of the strippers in *Gypsy,* the story of sophisticated strip artist Gypsy Rose Lee. Creighton had appeared in many local musicals including Pajama Game at the long defunct Houston Little Theater. She has carried on with her career in Hollywood and was most recently seen as the choir director in *Sisters One* and *Sisters Two* with Whoopie Goldberg. She certainly didn't look the same.

Opera singer **Enzo Stuarti** starred in South Pacific which ran at the Houston Music theater while my mom was visiting from Chicago. Naturally, I invited her to the opening night party. I thought she would faint when Stuarti put us arm around her for a photo. It was one of her fondest experiences.

Stuarti is remembered from Broadway, concert halls and recordings and even appeared in a Raagu spaghetti sauce commercial saying, *That's-a-nice!.* He died in 2005.

Andy Devine was just that...divine. He was the perfect Captain Andy in *Showboat.* With his gravelly voice and warm personality, he won everyone over. As usual, I had to escort him on his rounds of the radio, television and newspaper interviews and, we had to stop for lunch.

This time it was at Valhalla's in Houston's Old Market Square which was being revived in the 60s (the first time). The restaurant featured Greek food and had a real ship's hull as its centerpiece. We also stopped by Toni and Ernie Criszes' place, a deli style restaurant with music, just to show him how diversified nightlife was on the Square.

Unfortunately, the Market Square momentum plummeted within a year and the area is still struggling to come back.

This Was Burlesque was one of the last musicals I promoted for the Houston Music Theater. The show was a throwback to the old vaudeville days with comedians, singers and starring veteran strip tease artist **Ann**

Corio. She was no chicken, but she still looked good and liked to talk about some of her peers: "They've all had tummy tucks, face and butt lifts...but not me. What you see is what you get," she bragged. And it wasn't bad.

Corio had a long successful career on stage and made the transition to Hollywood and television, appearing in a few B pictures, most notably *Jungle Siren*, from the 40s to the early 60's. She introduced *This Was Burlesque,* to the stage in 1965 which ran for more than thirty years on and off-Broadway and toured across the country stopping at the Houston Music Theater in the late 60s.

Ann Corio followed her Broadway production with her *This Was Broadway* book recounting her memories of burlesque. She died in 1999 at age 84. Corio is a member of the Hall of Fame at the Exotic World Burlesque Museum in Leneldale, California.

Mitzi Gaynor did a great variety show at the Houston Music Theater. She and husband, Jack Bean, were a joy to work with. Bean was also her manager and they made a good team. Instead of bringing them to the KTRK-TV Morning Show studio, show hostess Jan Glenn came to the theater for the interview dressed in tap shoes and rehearsal costume. She didn't interview. She put herself into the act and bucked-and-winged, audition style. Mitzi and Jack just laughed and went along with her scheme. Hated to see them leave. They invited me to join them in California, but I knew they didn't really mean it.

Sammy Davis Jr., Ray Price, Sophia Loren and a few others made appearances at the Houston Music Theater which closed and reopened a couple of times after I left. It's been closed now for quite some years.

While still at Weekley and Valenti, I was contacted by Dr. A. Roy Price, a chemical engineer with the Merichem Company. They were thinking about hiring a public relations firm but were not yet ready to commit. Price was just screening agencies and getting some ideas. Soon after I opened R.Z. Estes,Inc., I got another call. This time, it was urgent.

John Files, Merichem's founder and president, had been appointed to the Texas Air Quality Board by then Governer John Connally. On that same day, my friend City Councilman Johnny Goyen announced his *Polluters of the Month* list on the front page of the Houston Chronicle. Merichem was Number One. State representatives vetoed Files' appointment and

Merichem was in an embarrassing situation that could very negatively affect their business reputation.

Reporters were storming the offices wanting a statement that they could print regarding the matter. The company's usual answer to controversy was "No comment," Dr. Price was frantic. "What do we do now?"

Well, the best thing the press wants to hear is "No comment". Then they can say whatever they want and simply end their story with: "When asked for a statement, the company had no comment!"

Files was out of town at the time, so I wrote a simple statement and had him phone the media from Chicago. It seemed that whenever anyone in the Merichem area smelled something unpleasant, because of its past bad publicity, they always blamed Merichem, which most times was not guilty.

So we made friends with city and county officials, invited them to the plant, showed them how it operated and controlled its emissions and kept them updated on anti-pollution measures through a bi-monthly newsletter.

Then I cooked up a community project for them. Because Buffalo Bayou in downtown Houston was still regarded as a cesspool, even though it was only murky with suspended silt and not actually polluted, I got Dr. Price and the Texas Society of Chemical Engineers to test the water and try to clarify it. Thus, the Pollution Solution Committee was formed.

After months of research, the engineers came up with an oil refinery by-product that would coagulate silt, the major culprit in the bayou's appearance, and clarify the water so that you could read beer can labels at the bottom. The product was free and the only expense would be aerating it into the water.

To make a point and educate the public, Dr. Price and I would go on television talk shows with a large beaker of murky bayou water. Price would then inject a few drops of the magic potion into the water; all of the silt would settle to the bottom. For the finale, we dropped in a gold fish who swam around happy and healthy proving that the water was safe. Hokey, yes. Did it work? YES! Houston's Polluter of the Month became Community Hero of the Month.

It was around the Fourth of July, the perfect time for a celebration and a real demonstration of the new found bayou Pollution Solution. We needed a place and some way to aerate the magic substance into the water. Since the Heritage Society park with restored historic homes was located downtown at one end of the Bayou, it was the perfect place for the event. The city fire department had the equipment to aerate the water and agreed to participate.

Peter Rippe, Heritage Society director, had never allowed a public event in "his park". But I talked him into it, explaining how important it was to connect the history of the bayou as it originally was to modern times. It could still be the center of recreation as it was in the early days when canoes floated down the bayou and a tight wire acrobat performed on the Heritage Society grounds. Rippe finally agreed and became a good friend and supporter.

The event was a tremendous success and continued for a few years when it was sponsored by another one of my clients, KHOU-TV, located across from Buffalo Bayou. It was one of my first experiences in booking free talent to entertain and I made contact with lots of local musicians and singers who were willing to participate for the publicity. It also put me in touch with the Daughters of the Republic of Texas, a group of descendants from the founders of the Republic of Texas, who became really good friends and dressed in their early Texas costumes to add history to many of my public events.

Peter Rippe eventually left Houston and the city outgrew our informal family Fourth of July celebration. I understand that the current Houston do-gooders are again looking for a way to clarify Buffalo Bayou. The Pollution Solution remedy might be just what they are looking for and it's been available for over forty years. And already approved by the state.

It was rumored that Marriott Hotels was planning to open its second Texas hotel in Houston. Dallas had the first which was a high end destination hotel for big expense account business travelers. Because Houston did not then have the commercial clout of Dallas, Marriott leaders decided that this hotel should appeal more directly to the community. It was located just a stone's throw from the new Astrodome and was opening at about the same time as the nearby NASA Space Station began operations with many purveyors moving to the site.

I called my friend, Councilman Johnny Goyen and he confirmed the rumor and agreed to put in a good word for me. He made some phone calls, and I made contact with the Aaron Cushman agency in Chicago, which coordinated all of Marriott's public relations satellite agencies. I made a presentation focusing on community involvement, was interviewed several times and finally got the account.

Because of its prime location, just a few blocks from the Astrodome, I planned tie-ins with events there that would bring locals as well as tourists to the hotel. it was still illegal to sell liquor by the drink in Texas so my biggest challenge was to develop a draw for the Sirloin & Saddle Lounge. As the name implied, it had a western theme in décor, food and live entertainment. Almost every venue coming to Houston at that time imagined every city in Texas as the "old west" and wanted to include cowboys and Indians in their projects. Actually, Houston was very far from "old west" and was trying to discourage that image.

In order to serve liquor legally, we had to form a private club with a prominent board of directors who would attract new members. About this time the original **Mercury Seven astronauts** were moving to Houston to prepare for NASA's first manned spacecraft liftoff which would be controlled from the Houston Space Center.

John Glenn and **Scott Carpenter** are the only ones of the original seven astronauts still alive. Those looking down upon us are **Gordon Cooper, Gus Grissom, Wally Schirra, Alan Shepard** and **Deke Slayton**. They were most cooperative and their wives agreed to model in charity fashion shows that Clear Lake City sponsored.

Official coordinator for the astronauts and all of the other NASA related staff was **Grace Winn**, an incredible, warm caring native Houstonian who accidentally "fell" into her assignment as NASA's "official greeter" while visiting her friend Congressman Olin E. "Tiger" Teague at his Washington, DC office. She was recovering from an auto accident and took advantage of the down time to travel to D. C., one of her favorite places to visit her influential transplanted Houston friends.

Actually, "greeter" was a misnomer. Winn was responsible for making the newcomers feel at home in Houston. She met NASA personnel at the airport, entertained them, helped them find housing, introduced them to shopping, schools and the best Houston had to offer. She quickly became irreplaceable and the epitomy of Houston hospitality.

Grace Winn became a good friend after just a few weeks and the bonus for me was invitations to many of the snazzy parties at prominent bayside mansions and special events like the after show party for **Carol Channing**. Grace introduced us after her show at Jones Hall and she was delightful. Got to see Channing again at the Houston Country Playhouse where she did her fantastic one-woman show.

I envisioned the Mercury Seven as the nucleus of the Sirloin & Saddle board and called Winn to present the idea. She loved it. Of course J. W. Marriott was no stranger to the political game which indirectly affected his relationship with NASA. His hospitality was recognized as the best. Half the battle had already been won. Not only did Marriott get the astronauts on their Sirloin & Saddle board, the hotel was also booked for the exciting Splash Down parties following moon landings and other NASA related special events.

Most of the entertainment at the Sirloin & Saddle was handled through Marriott's national booking agency which moved acts throughout their circuit. A favorite was **Ray Frushay,** a nationally acclaimed rockabilly/country performer and songwriter who lived in Austin, Texas.

Talented, handsome and friendly, he was a dream to work with and I secretly had a crush on him. He was married, had two daughters, but was estranged from them because of his lengthy road trips. But he loved them.

Frushay came back to the Marriott-Astrodome several times, had released a couple of record albums and was preparing to write some new songs to tape for another album. Sam Cammarata was his manager, which became his downfall. Cammarata took control of Frushay's new tapes, locked them up and calmed the furious Ray down with drugs which he eventually became addicted to. Cammarata put him into a rehab facility to keep him out of the public eye.

A couple of years later, Ray gave me a call. He came to the house with his guitar and I hardly recognized him. He had gained weight, was unkempt and looked terrible. The famous Ray Frushay was a lost soul. He asked me to help him get back in the Marriott as a single, but they were not interested.

However, former Marriott catering manager Ron Jordon had gotten the franchise for the Quality Inn-Airport and agreed to use Ray for the cocktail hour. Jordan gave him money to buy some new clothes and a haircut. Ray started a new, downscaled career. But it didn't last. He didn't show up a couple of times and Jordon had to let him go.

I never heard from Ray Frushay again. His daughter, Sheri has followed in his footsteps and become a popular singer on her own, especially loved in Europe. She won Singer of the Year Award ICMAG in Germany. Sheri Frushay's newest CD, *Scarlet Song* was supported and encouraged by Austin musician/artist Butch Hancock.

Ray Frushay's albums are still available on line and include some of his best songs like *Something On My Mind*, *Please Just Say So* and *Cheatin' Traces* which is still being played on country radio around the country. He played Officer Smith in *Ransom Money,* an obscure movie released in 1970. Retired from the business, Ray still lives in Texas and occasionally joins some of his friends with his guitar.

The Seoul Sisters, five Korean cuties who loved garlic, made a big hit at the Sirloin & Saddle with their rendition of "Sugar Sugar". Before each performance, they would raid the kitchen and stock up on their favorite food, fresh garlic. Not too good for patrons near the stage. They were a peppy appealing group with lots of spunk.

B. J. Thomas was another Sirloin & Saddle favorite. He was so cooperative and agreed to do a radio commercial with his famous *Raindrops Are Falling on My Head* as the background music to promote his appearance at the Sirloin & Saddle.

Occasionally, Marriott-Astrodome allowed me to bring in local talent. One such group came from Astroworld. Two guys, two girls and a backup trio. They had been performing singly, but I put them together as a group. We named them **Future Faces.** They became regulars on the Marriott club circuit. Two of the four were already a couple. The other two became more than chums on the road. Unfortunately, the friendship that brought them all together became the wedge that divided them. Future Faces were in the past in less than a year.

The Rhodes Kids was a Houston family group including mom and pop and their offspring with the youngest around five years old wowing audiences with *Jeremiah Was a Bullfrog.* Don't know what happened to them.

When business was slow, but we still needed entertainment, we found an accordionist who was very versatile. The Club introduced a series of European themed nights matching the food to the music. The accordionist complied; he changed hats and accent to match the theme. But the music was always the same.

Two of the funniest comics were not on the Sirloin & Saddle stage, but in the Marriott kitchen. Sirloin & Saddle manager Helmut Stuhlman, a tall good looking German hunk, and Swiss Chef Lucas delivered unbelievable dialog in the kitchen, screaming obscenities in two different languages and punctuating the discussion by throwing raw eggs at each other. Never know what goes on behind closed kitchen doors. There were always smiles up front.

When it came to getting publicity, however, they worked together. When Ann Valentine, Houston food editor, wanted a Christmas setup in October, we found the appropriate decorations and recipes. When she wanted a luau theme in March, Stuhlman cut branches from the palm trees around the pool, upsetting the general manager, and set up a Hawaiian table with food to match. That kind of exposure is not possible today. Whatta shame.

To celebrate Mardi Gras in Houston, I suggested bringing in a parade Krewe from Louisiana. The **Krewe of Jupiter**, who annually marched in the New Orleans parade, hailed from Crawley, Louisiana. Many Houstonians had never seen the elaborate costumes and headdresses designed for Mardi Gras days and their visit brought in many curious customers.

The Krewe reciprocated by inviting Marriott manager Ted Wright, wife Rachel and me as guests to the actual Krewe celebration in New Orleans. It was my first visit to Louisiana and the event was amazing. The town fathers also invited me back to judge a Rice Queen beauty competition in Crawley which was most unusual.

After viewing all of the beauties, we judges agreed on the winner...but she wasn't the right one. The pageant committee had a different idea, held an impromptu meeting and in a few minutes, their pre-elected Rice Queen choice was announced. Seems beauty runs more than skin deep in Crawley, Louisiana.

San Antonio's **Jim Cullum** and his Dixieland Band which played at The Landing on the developing River Walk were also featured at the Sirloin & Saddle along with some Flamingo dancers and other entertainers from the San Antonio River Walk, vintage 1970. The original **Dukes of Dixieland** were also a popular one week stand.

Winding down the live entertainment era, Marriott national sent down *The Best of Broadway*, a semi-talented foursome who performed mini renditions of popular Broadway musicals. Actually they weren't that talented and we decided to try a group from a local theater. It didn't work either, so canned music took over.

The Sirloin & Saddle, however, was not the only action spot at the Marriott-Astrodome. Again, because of J. W. Marriott's fantastic contacts – he had started his business with a small hamburger stand in Washington, D.C., -- we got lots of VIP galas.

The **Bob Hope** birthday party which was officially celebrated at the Astrodome wound up at the Marriott with almost as much star power as the Shamrock Hotel opening night. Organized by wannabe socialite Mary Jo Bell (who always wore her wig backwards because she said it had more body that way), the event attracted many of Hope's friends including **Frank Sinatra** and his then new wife Barbara, **Robert Goulet, Dean Martin,** and **Dorothy Lamour**.

Congressman **George H. W. Bush**, as head of the United Nations, hosted annual birthday parties for that organization while sons young (now president) George and Jeb fidgeted, sometimes not so quietly, in the lobby.

Ladies of the evening also vied for star billing at the the Marriott, as they do in most hotels. Security spotted them and escorted them to the door. It was my job to quiet the incidents. Sometimes no news is good news.

Impressing the press was another objective for the Marriott-Astrodome and I hosted regular "nights out" at the Sirloin & Saddle. Budget was always a consideration at the Club and Manager Stuhlman had hesitated to purchase more saute pans for flaming dishes. There were only two. His reasoning was that rarely more than two order a flaming dish at the same time. But that changed one evening when four of the press guests ordered flambe and there were only two pans. Stuhlman ordered two more the next day.

Special promotions also came to the Marriott-Astrodome including the Lark Cigarettes hot air balloon which I got to ride in, but not for very far. Houston doesn't have much balloon weather. Also hosted a gumbo cook-off on the parking lot. If it looked like a good news event event... Marriott-Astrodome went for it.

Working with the Marriott was, like Anheuser-Busch, being a part of a family. And it wasn't all work and no play. Periodically management would arrange in-house or outside parties including a really fun time on a borrowed boat sailing on the Houston ship channel. The hotel's opening manager was Paul Reed. He and wife Sue hosted the event. They were fantastic people. Reed eventually became a senior officer at Marriott headquarters.

Ted Wright was a memorable second manager. He was comparatively young, good looking and came from the Marriott resort in Scottsdale, Arizona. Although he was happily married to a very lovely lady, he had an eye for young beauties. When **Ryan O'Neal** and **Jacqueline Bisset** stayed at the hotel while filming *The Thief Who Came to Dinner*, shot mostly at the Astrodome and in River Oaks traditional-old wealth mansions, Wright lusted after Bisset. His biggest kick was setting up wet tee shirt contests around the hotel pool, always urging Bisset to compete. She never did.

In addition to all of the public events at the Marriott, there were many celebrity one-timers. Singer **Jack Jones** had his fifth (I think) wedding in the lobby.

Roy Rogers, a Marriott friend, opened his first Houston Roy Rogers Roast Beef restaurant next to the second Houston Marriott at the Galleria on Westheimer. He was easy to talk to and related how he spent a lot of time in the barn at the back of his ranch to get a reprieve from Dale in the main house. Don't think it was always Happy Trails for them.

Sid Ceasar came in for a personal appearance and his press conference might still be going on if everyone had not decided that almost two hours was too long and excused themselves. Ceasar was delightful and loved to talk and talk and talk. He was always funny.

Baseball great **Yogi Berra** held his press conference to promote Yahoo Chocolate Drink at the Marriott. He was lots of fun, a great interview and still lives in Houston where he was an Astros coach until 1994. His clever Yogi-isms were compiled in a book, one of several Berra wrote.

Marriott-Astrodome hosted the Miami Dolphin and Minnesota Viking players in the 1974 Super Bowl which was played in the nearby Rice Stadium, the first neutral grounds in Super Bowl history. Miami won against the Vikings 24 to 7, but everybody was happy at the Marriott after game party. Packing the lobby to meet and greet the players, fans got a special treat. **Joe Namath** had come to watch the game and caused a riot among the young ladies in the audience. He was awesome.

In addition to hotels, Marriott had many tourist related holdings including the Stella Solaris Greek cruise lines which was scheduled to come to Houston. To attract local interest, I encouraged them to dock the ship at the Port of Houston and move it to Galveston for its maiden voyage from Texas to the Carribbean islands. We hosted a charity event on board and it then sailed to its exotic island destinations.

The Houston Zoo was planning a big fund raising event and I suggested they hold it aboard the Stella Solaris. It was an amazing party, attracted hundreds of people, raised lots of money for the zoo and set the stage for cruising from Galveston and Houston. Now very popular with many other cruise lines, ships regularly sail out of Houston and Galveston.

Among the entertainers on board the Stella Solaris was a group of five young men from New York...***The***

20th Century. I made the Stella Solaris maiden voyage from Houston with my daughter, Victoria, and the talented guys made the trip fun. Bored with life on board, we jumped ship and spent a night on land in Cancun. They taught the Hustle at a few of the popular discos there and we all joined in. We hated to leave.

One of the Houston passengers fell in love with the 20th Century and booked them for a Houston fund raiser at Jones Hall. They were ecstatic, but were on a tight budget and couldn't afford a hotel stay. I put them up at our place. Housing five male singers from New York city was certainly different. **Red Skelton** and **Helen Redding** were that show's headliners. Skelton was great; Redding was late. And not so great.

As Houston grew, Marriott wanted to increase its presence in the city's new trendy part of town, the Galleria on Westheimer. The Marriott-Galleria opened in the early 1970s with a real splash. Getting front page coverage from daily papers was never easy, but that's what we were aiming for. The opening event had to be spectacular from invitation to the grand opening party.

Again, Marriott wanted to go back to the Old West. I designed an invitation that would be branded in leather, rolled, tied with thong and delivered by scouts on horseback, pony express style. No printer could print on leather so I found a photographer who said he could "brand" the invitation, one by one...he thought.

Actually, he thought wrong. The leather fibers gummed up the branding iron and smeared the lettering. So he found a silk screener in the neighborhood who could do the job to look authentic without that much elbow grease. However, some of the Marriott chiefs wanted to see the branding process so decided to visit the photographer's studio to watch. That was a hard one to get out of, but the invitations turned out great, were a big hit with everyone. No one was the wiser.

About the splash. Marriott-Galleria had an indoor swimming pool flanked by five stories of rooms with balconies. I got the idea to get someone to dive from a fifth floor balcony into the pool which would then set off 500 balloons flying in the air from the adjoining atrium.

A young diving coach at the University of Houston agreed to do the job and even offered to set his body on fire as an added attraction. He had worked in water shows in Florida and was confident that there would be no problem. When the time came, he jumped, body in flames and hit the water with the big splash we were all expecting. He was truly shaken up, wobbling out of the pool. I don't think he ever tried that stunt again.

The jump made front page of the Houston Post, and set the course for Marriott's ongoing success in Houston.

David Marriott, a J. W. Marriott nephew, was the first manager of the Houston-Galleria. He was a strange duck with none of J.W.'s flair. His biggest thrill was Halloween. He ordered all of the staff to dress in costume, including himself, and parade around the property. Doesn't take much to make some people happy. But not everyone.

Don't know what happened to that David Marriott, but J. W's son, Bill, was on the scene observing operations in preparation for his eventual takeover. Hard to believe that he was practically a "youngster" then. Today, he is in his 70's and his 34-year old son, David, is training to take over the reins and introducing new concepts and theories to the corporation.

While I was with them, Marriott was also testing hospitality opportunities in foreign lands. The Marriott-Acapulco was among their first out of the country efforts. They purchased an existing property in Acapulco's downtown tourist area and opened it as the

Acapulco Marriott, Since I was "in the neighborhood" they allowed me to promote it in Texas.

I invited my Houston media buddies to visit the Acapulco Marriott and got to spend three Thanksgivings with my three children there. That was real living. Since then, Marriott sold its original Acapulco hotel and has opened a couple of new ones there.

Because my late first husband was a news reporter for KTRK-TV(ABC) in Houston, I got to know the staff, particularly the talk show hosts, well enough to offer some guest ideas (from my clients) for their show. **Ed Ames**, of the famed Ames Brothers quartet, hosted the Morning Show for quite a while in the early 70s. Marriott chefs often did food demonstrations which were always popular with audiences and the camera crew. They would prepare a recipe and offer the finished product for sampling. The crew was always hungry.

Some of the stars I met while waiting for my people to go on air included a very young **John Travolta** straight from his success in Grease. **Ann Margaret,** who was really cute in spite of her acne, shocked everyone with her sailor mouth. The **Ames Brothers** made regular appearances with their brother Ed on his show.

Marvin Zindler was the station's consumer advocate. The son of a Houston retail clothing legend, Zindler hated the business and wanted to be a newsman. For a while, he freelanced with local stations, pushing some of the regulars out of the way while he sensationalized the news. Many of the reporters at the time remember when a plane crashed just outside of Houston. It was a real disaster with bodies scattered in all directions. Reporters were covering the event with taste and sympathy.

Zindler brought on-the-spot drama to the situation. Rumor has it that he was interviewing a near-death victim who had been moaning. "We're right on the scene and this poor man is in the midst of death groans. You can hear him now..." Zindler reported. The man had passed out, but that didn't phase Marvin, he gave him a kick and the moans began. An unforgettable experience.

Zindler later became a regular consumer advocate reporter for KTRK-TV, investigating frauds, injustice...and prostitution. He somehow hit on the legendary Chicken Ranch, a known house of prostitution frequented by Texas A & M students and local law officials. He researched the operation, tipped local authorities and orchestrated the raid that closed the place down. The result: *The Best Little Whorehouse in Texas* which premiered at Houston's converted Alabama Theater with local songstress June Terry as the Madam and Marvin Zindler...as himself. Better than Broadway!

KHOU-TV (CBS) retained R. Z. Estes, Inc. in the early 70s to handle its public relations adding another dimension to the agency, working FOR as well as with media.

Joanne King, the international socialite played by Julia Roberts in the *Charlie Wilson's War* movie based on the book by George Crile, appeared on her first channel 11 daily noon show as a one time effort to raise money for one of her charities. Viewer response to her was so positive that manager Dean Borba offered her a permanent job hosting the **Joanne King Show** every day at noon.

An only child raised on the outskirts of River Oaks, Houston's old wealth neighborhood, Joanne was persuasive, opinionated and curious from childhood and craved wealth, international recognition and excitement. King loved politics and always wanted to be involved with causes that counted for the betterment of humanity and the poor around the world, unlike the image she projected as a beautiful, clingy, not too smart southern belle.

Pursued by many boys-to-men all through school because of her exceptional beauty and interesting mind, Joanne Johnson opted to drop her University of Texas studies and marry up and coming real estate developer Robert King in 1949.

The Kings lived in a large, sparsely furnished house in River Oaks, her familiar old mansion-filled neighborhood. It was the scene of their much publicized Roman Toga party in 1959 which Bob King put together for Joanne's thirtieth birthday setting the stage for the rest of her life – attracting international attention.

By nature a quiet man, Bob King outdid himself with this party that fascinated the world through an expansive Life magazine pictorial spread. It looked almost like a Roman orgy. It gave Joanne the notoriety she craved, though not as classy as she would have liked.

As channel 11's public relations consultant, I worked with Joanne King to get other media publicity for her new show which ran for fifteen years, long after I was gone. Always interested in foreigners and foreign policy

King had courted some of Europe's finest struggling and dethroned royalty and attracted them to Houston with glamorous parties and the promise of a greater identity in the states.

Having scheduled a story on one of these events for the society section of the Houston Chronicle, I arrived at the house early to check out photo possibilities. Joanne and her staff-for-the-day were testing the antique but not reinforced chairs around the dining table to determine which would hold the heaviest guests. Name tags were placed according to the guest's weight.

When party time came the caterers frantically tried to find utensils, serving tables and other necessities normally expected in a kitchen (but weren't there) while a young **George Hamilton,** a Hollywood guest, surveyed the scene with amusement. We chatted and laughed. Hamilton was a quiet man with a great sense of humor.

The catering staff finally found a small rusty rolling table with wobbly wheels outside at the pool that would have to do as a server. When I turned in the story, Chronicle society editor Betty Ewing discovered another problem. Joanne was wearing a tight, light weight white dress that revealed ALL when the photographer's flash bulb went off. It took a lot of retouching to make that photo avoid an X-rating.

While the party was in full swing Robert King, who by now was living in the guest house out back, made an appearance in jeans and tee shirt getting everyone's attention, especially wife Joanne's. He was not expected. Actually, according to an article by Claudia Feldman in the Houston Chronicle, Bob King's idea of heaven was living on a desert island; Joanne King's dream was to live around the world in a whirl of excitement and adventure.

Joanne and Robert King divorced soon after and she was a single mom until1972 when she met and married her *soul mate*, millionaire oilman Robert Herring, who shared her love of travel, politics, beautiful things and excitement. Through his extensive travels which Joanne shared with her husband, Herring kept abreast of the world's problems and was introduced to the disturbing situation between Afghanistan and Russia.

Joanne's unmatched influence over royalty and high society as well as decision-making politicians was obvious round the world resulting in her appointments as honorary consul to Pakistan and to Morocco and volunteer head of an organization to revamp Pakistani handcrafts to appeal to the western market. Her efforts were too successful. Politicians and middlemen immediately recognized the financial potential and skimmed profits off the top instead of sharing with the poor villagers as she had intended. King resigned.

Possibly preventing what she believed to be a Soviet take over of the world, Joanne Herring put on her reporter cap and slipped into Afghanistan, interviewing tribal warriors with her professional combat photographer son, Robin. Experienced filmmaker Charles Fawcett directed their efforts showing helicopter attacks and vicious hand-to-hand combat. The final film was shown to influential politicians and decision makers everywhere to make an impact and gain support.

Robert Herring died of lung cancer in 1981, but Joanne King Herring carried on his crusade, attracting Texas playboy Congressman Charlie Wilson as an ally. He was captivated by her charm and determination. In his position on the Appropriations Committee, Wilson was able to channel billions of American dollars to aid Afghanistan's war efforts against the Soviet Union. The result of their short lived love and war affair was a free

Afghanistan and an eventually free Charlie Wilson who is now married and living in Lubbeck.

Born in July, 1929, still beautiful and shapely with a little help from plastic surgery, Joanne King Herring Davis is as adventurous as ever. Living in a deluxe condo in her ever-familiar River Oaks neighborhood, she is a credit to Houston, the nation and the world.

KHOU-TV station manager Dean Borba had another type of fixation. He was fascinated by Texas' first Mrs. America, **Joy Noufer**, when he first saw her in the pageant on television. She was vivacious, charming and talented in homemaking chores which is why she won. Borba immediately wanted her to host a morning show even though she had absolutely no on-air or acting experience. The choice proved profitable.

Viewers identified with the Morning Show hostess who was a prizewinning homemaker. There was even a movie, *Joy in the Morning,* which previewed at the River Oaks Theater. As a special tribute to Noufer, Borba claimed she was truly *Joy in the Morning.* The station hosted a preview party in her honor at the River Oaks Theater.

Joy had been married for some time to Chuck Noufer. a naïve easy going guy who adored her. They had three children and seemed an ideal couple. We attended many dinners at her home and she was a favorite at the Marriott's Sirloin & Saddle, especially with manager Helmut Stuhlman. Rumors were flying that there was something more than employer-employee relations going on between Borba and Noufer. Seems that his car was seen parked in front of her home during the day while Chuck was at work.

They finally confirmed the rumors, left their partners (Chuck was in shock) and were married. The new Borbas were guests at the Acapulco Marriott on their honeymoon. However, Noufer's show was getting a little shakey and finally ended. She was gaining weight and the newlyweds were not nearly as happy as they were before the nuptials. I saw Joy once after that at a social event and she really had gotten big. Shortly thereafter, she died of undetermined causes. This time, the second time around wasn't better.

Television news reporter **Jessica Savitch** came to KHOU-TV in the early 1970s and was a relentless news hound, beating the pants off the male reporters. I publicized her arrival and we became friends, cruising around after hours looking for excitement. Savitch was short termer at KHOU. In no time she was snatched up by the NBC network and became one of the most successful news anchorwomen ever. Jessica was recovering from many personal problems including drugs and failed loves when she was killed in a tragic automobile accident in 1983. A real tragedy.

On a Clear Day poster with Linda Lavin and Van Johnson. By Hap Garman.

Ann Corio in This Was Burlesque at the Houston Music Theater.

At home with Van Johnson

Devine lunch with Andy (Captain Andy) Devine.

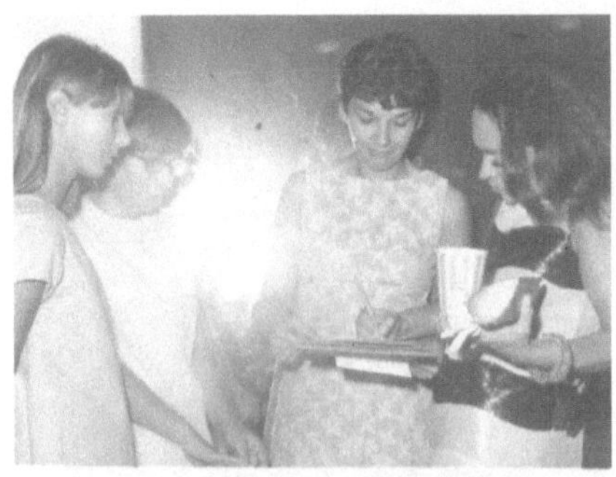

Sound of Music's Patrice Munsel autographs a photo for my stars, Viki and Lori.

Economic Summit, Houston Texas.

Rockabilly singer Ray Frushay wowed them at the Houston Marriott Astrodome's Sirloin & Saddle Club

Jessica Savitch left Houston's KHOU-TV to become a national news celebrity.

CHAPTER 9

Short Termers

I worked with Marriott Hotels and the Merichem Company for over fifteen years and almost as long with KHOU-TV giving the agency a steady cash flow over a long period of time. Some clients, however were "short termers"... five years or less. Others were handled on a one-time consulting basis. I worked with Astroworld for about three years. The late 1960s and 70's business seemed to be focused on tourism and tourist attractions rather than strippers, stars and presidents. Times were changing.

Houstonians and visitors alike flipped over Astroworld when it opened in June, 1968. Sidney Schlenker, then still associated with PACE Management as well as director of the Astrodome complex which included Astroworld, suggested that I take over the publicity and public relations for the park instead of an in-house person. Astroworld manager George Lanier, nephew of Bob Lanier who became a Houston mayor, agreed and hired me. It was the beginning of a continuous roller coaster ride.

Judge Roy Hofheinz was involved with the theme park from the beginning as a part of his Astrodomain complex, which he named in honor of the astro-connected Johnson Space Center announced for Houston in 1965. A former Harris County Judge, he hung on to the title throughout his flamboyant career. Hofheinz had collected many antique theme park artifacts and donated some of them to Astroworld including a vintage Dentzel Carousel located in the Alpine Valley area of the park which also included the popular Alpine Sleigh ride.

Designer Gustav Dentzel brought a carousel from his father's Dentzel Carousel Company in Germany to America in the mid-1800s. The Astroworld version was built in 1902 and operated steadily until 2005 when Astroworld closed. It was put on the market in 2006 and purchased by Dan Horenberger, Brass Ring entertainment, saving it from auction and possible dismanteling.

Some of the Judge's other collectibles went into his surreal penthouse suite at the Astroworld Hotel. Spread over several rooms, each space had its own theme. The Jungle Room was most awesome with heads of wild animals and exotic furnishings. VIP guests were invited to enjoy cocktails in his penthouse and visitors were allowed to tour it on special occasions.

George Lanier was a serious young man with lots of imagination which he injected into the creation and naming of park rides and characters. He dreamed up Marvel McVey, the Mickey Mouse of Astroworld, who greeted park guests and made personal appearances. He was outlandish in appearance dressed in bright pink and orange and turquoise. His costume was pure fantasy with a giant pink feather decorated hat. A munchkin/pirate combination.

Because of his unusual creativity, Lanier was invited to Paris, France to consult on a version of Astroworld for that city. Lanier died in the early 70s, rumored, by suicide.

The Dexter Freebish Electric Roller Ride (named by Lanier and renamed Excalibur in 1981)) was introduced in the County Fair section of Astroworld in 1972. Built by Arrow Dynamics, their first all steel structure, it was higher and different from the mine trains the company had built for Six Flags Over Texas in Dallas. Dexter was a three-element coaster: the Dip, the Spiral and the Pit Curve and was believed to be a forerunner to Arrow's

299-foot plus Hypercoasters. This unique coaster ride continued to be a favorite until the Park closed.

Originally covering 57 acres (later expanded to more than 75 acres) across the highway from the Astrodome, Astroworld opened with eight different themed areas. Western Junction was my favorite because it included the Crystal Palace with live shows and budding stars who went on to national fame.

Ventriloquist **Jay Johnson** was featured at Astroworld and Six Flag parks across the country while he was still in high school and was on the same bill as the members of Marriott Hotel's Future Faces who performed individually at the Crystal Palace. In the mid-70's, Jay moved to Los Angeles to pursue his ideas for television which resulted in network and HBO specials, hundreds of guest appearances and a four-year recurring role on *Soap*, a camp TV series which still runs in syndication around the world. Johnson is passionate about his art and has created shows that delve into the mystery of ventriloquism including his most successful touring show *The Two and Only* examining the relationship between the ventriloquist and his "partner".

For thrills at Astroworld, I got to stand up on the roller coaster to assist photographers get "just the right angle", greet and tour VIP guests like **Lorna Luft** and **Liza Minnelli** who came with Houston Chronicle columnist Maxine Messinger and create and deliver news and investigate the only disaster to occur while I was there, a lady falling off a ride while it was in motion. It was all part of my job. I managed to get Astroworld featured on the first color cover of Southwest Airlines' Inflight magazine adding to the Park's national reputation. Astroworld was the best "family friendly" account I ever had. My kids loved it and so did I!

While Minnelli and Luft were in Houston that year, they also visited another of my clients, the Continental Houston hotel which opened across from Allen's Landing on Buffalo Bayou and was managed by Bill Click. European immigrants landed at Allen's Landing in 1836 with the Allen Brothers, believing they were at the Port of Galveston. The brothers purchased some land, sold it to settlers and thus, Houston was born at Allen's Landing. The city flourished in the 1880s and early 1900s as a railroad center. Many of the German immigrants opened watch repair shops to service the railroad workers who depended upon their timepieces to run the railroad.

Sweeney's Jewelers, an S. L. Brown account, was one of those originals. Founded in 1881 by fellow I. & G.N. Railroad workers J. J. Sweeney and Eden L. Coombs, Sweeney-Coombs Jewelry store moved into its namesake building at Main and Congress in 1889. One of Houston's remaining Victorian style structures, it was designed by prominent architect Eugene Heiner who designed many of the buildings in the area including one across from Market Square that later housed the famed Sonny Look's Depot restaurant. It was demolished in the '70s by the Bank of Commerce. Sweeney and Coombs diverted from jewelry to real estate and developed the first park on Buffalo Bayou at the current site of the Houston Heritage Society's Sam Houston Park which displays examples of early 19th century homes.

According to legend, at 3 o'clock every Sunday afternoon at the park, a lady named Mrs. Roaming floated up in a hot air balloon with a monkey on her shoulder. There was a goat race track and canoes paddled up and down Buffalo Bayou. The pair also owned the Sweeney-Coombs Opera House, Houston's first theater which opened in 1891 with the Graus Opera Company's presentation of *The Gondoliers.* Sweeney's Jewelry is still in business serving the nation with high quality gems. I wrote the history of the company for its 75th anniversary in 1956. It celebrated its 125th anniversary in 2006.

Judy Garland's daughters and Maxine Messinger arrived at the Continental Houston in the middle of a performance by star attraction, vocalist **Jaye P. Morgan,** who had delayed her show waiting for them. When the audience became loudly impatient, she began singing. Then, the trio stomped into the room stumbling and talking while Jaye P. tried to ignore the confusion. Maxine introduced their arrival with a loud..."Welcome to the Shitrock!" Jaye P. was shocked, but went on with her performance. That was a big show stopper.

However, after checking into Mary Margaret Morgan's biography (she was nicknamed Jaye P. by her high school classmates after J. P. Morgan the banker), I found that Jaye P. had become a little racy on her own. She had just gotten divorced when she played the Continental and seemed very quiet and withdrawn. We drove together to her media interviews and I took her to see a new house I was building. On the way, we had a little fender bender which resulted in a ticket which we agreed I didn't deserve.

Morgan kept out of the public eye for a couple of years after that and returned to attract a new generation of TV fans, especially on the raunchy Playboy Channel game show *Everything Goes,* with her off-color off-the-cuff remarks. Often bleeped during her appearances on *The Gong Show*, the reborn Morgan was caught flashing Gene-Gene, The Dancing Machine character on the show, by removing her blouse....more than once. Rumor has it she was asked to leave the show...forever. A far cry from the timid shy Jaye P. Morgan I remember from the Continental-Houston.

The Continental housed name stars once in a while. **Eddy Arnold** was a Houston Rodeo favorite and played the arena in 1951, 53, 60, 64, 67, 72 and 82. He stayed at the Continental Houston in 1972 and we got to talk over old times going back to his Wichita concert when Colonel Tom Parker was his manager. He was more charming than ever and had evolved from the Grand Ole Opry Tennessee plowboy image to a sophisticated multi-faceted star singing pop and rock as well as country in concerts and night clubs, on records and at rodeos and fairs.

Colonel Parker had guided Arnold's successful career in the right direction in its first phase. Second manager Jerry Purcell followed his path, leading him in a broader direction to attract a new generation of fans. Arnold was inducted into the Country Music Hall in 1966. He sold over 85 million records with twenty-eight Number One hits on Billboard's Country Singles chart. Unlike many of his peers, Arnold stayed married to the same wife, Sally, for more than sixty years. She died in March of 2007 followed by Eddy in May. The Tennessee Plowboy was and always will be a true country gentleman. My favorite song of his has always been "The Tennessee Stud", which he did to perfection.

Being involved with the hospitality and entertainment industries in the mid-60s led to reuniting with Jim Battersby. Still in San Antonio, he was now the promoter for Texas Tourism with state tourism director Frank Nikimkin. San Antonio was preparing for its first-ever world class event – Hemisfair-1968 – which turned the city from a sleeping frog into a notable prince on the international tourist scene. The impressive 600 foot tall Tower of the Americas erected for the occasion beckoned visitors from far and wide to the city and its developing River Walk.

I was fortunate to sit in on the initial Hemisfair planning committee which led to new business prospects. As a matter of fact, business was getting so good that I needed to hire another person. Kathy Rhoads, a confident bright recent University of Texas journalism graduate, applied and joined our small staff. Her job was getting news tidbits out to the columnists, writing news releases, helping out at trade shows and chauffering clients to interviews.

Strippers and presidents were becoming scarce on the agency agenda, but there still were a few stars. Through Jim Battersby, I landed the Discover Texas account which involved selling Texas outside of the state and putting together a Texas type show to tour the country. Starring in that production were members of the **Alabama- Coushatta Indian** tribes headquartered on a reservation near Livingston, Texas. They were to perform "native" dances which they learned from a Boy Scout troupe since they had no history of dancing in their tribal background.

Laid back and not used to discipline, the troupe was often late and occasionally a no-show at some of these performances. Booked close to home at an Austin shopping mall, they were expected one day at noon.

The audience waited anxiously. Fifteen, thirty, forty-five minutes. Finally they gave up and left. About four days later, the Indians shuffled in. They didn't seem to think it made any difference if they came a little (?) late and wondered what happened to the stage and the audience.

To help them get on track, Battersby suggested to Roland Poncho, the tribes' marketing/public relations manager, that they hire me to work with them on their public image. The state had just built them a really nice amphitheater and worked with them to create a production that would bring visitors to the reservation. *Beyond the Sundown* was the story of the Indians' struggle for survival in Texas and was quite dramatic played under the stars. Publicity was aimed at bringing in an audience and enticing them to spend the night after the performance either in their own RV or a rustic cabin on the Reservation so they could take the nature walks and spend money at the restaurant and gift shop the next day.

Somehow, the Indian youths did not quite agree with that concept. On cool evenings, they would break into the cabins, take the wood furnishings and build a fire outside. Because they did not relish strangers infringing on their territory, they substituted the informtive Nature Trail signs with their own obscene versions, turning visitors away.

The final straw was the planned grand opening of a permanent Alabama-Coushatta history museum which told the tribes' story in pictures and artifacts. The tribes' symbol was the brilliant red cardinal and one of their most talented artists created one which was set in a place of honor in a glass showcase. However, the day before grand opening, the cardinal evidently flew the coop. The tribesmen knew who took it but, because of tradition, they could not accuse him.

Tribal custom dictates that members ignore a known thief until he voluntarily returns the stolen property. In the meantime, Roland Poncho moved to another reservation for several years and the museum remained closed. When he returned to manage the museum in the mid-1990s, he was able to locate the missing bird and finally have a grand opening.

Alabama-Coushatta young people were incredibly artistic: painting, sculpting and potting. But they lacked the self-confidence and interest to succeed and instead turned to mind altering substances to satisfy their needs. Operation Headstart was a positive addition and has had a remarkable influence on the younger children giving them and the tribes positive hopes for the future.

Attempting to extend the season, I put together a country music show to run in October at the Beyond the Sundown Theater. There was not much entertainment in the surrounding communities during the fall season and it would be an opportunity to attract local audiences as well as tourists. Pappy Selph, popular fiddler and author of "Orange Blossom Special", a rousing country fiddle tune, was the volunteer headliner. Lesser known locals completed the program.

After one performance, the effort was deemed a failure. Soon after, oil was discovered on the reservation. Beyond the Sundown was closed in 1983 and tourists were no longer necessary to help finance the Alabama-Coushatta Indian Reservation. I wasn't needed any more, either.

My mother, who was always star struck, got to have her picture taken with Pappy Selph and it was a day she never forgot. He even gave her a tape of his music. At one time, he played with the popular Light Crust Doughboys country western band.

The **Gilbert & Sullivan** Society of Houston was founded in 1952 by a small group of enthusiasts headed by Kinkaid School headmaster John Copper. Its premier production that year was *The Gondoliers,* the same musical that opened the Sweeney-Coombs Opera House many years earlier. It was presented at Cullen Auditorium on the University of Houston campus. I did their publicity from 1970 through 1979 covering rehearsals held at the Kinkaid auditorium and staging picnics and other events with the cast in full costume for publicity. At that time, the cast with family and friends constructed the sets and costumes for the show. Today, they have a warehouse filled with sets and costumes which is one of the most complete in the country and other companies come to borrow.

In 1966, the G&S Society took part in the opening ceremonies of Jones Hall, Houston's new symphony home and moved its productions to that venue. Vocal and technical scholarships were initiated from performance proceeds and Gulf Oil Corporation sponsored the Society's television production of *Princess Ida* in 1974 in conjunction with the Austin/Houston Public Broadcasting Systems, which earned an Emmy nomination that year.

With the closing of the D'Oyly Carte Opera Company in England in 1982, the Society gained one of its most prominent lead performers, Alistair Donkin, who has spent his summers in Houston ever since serving as both stage director and featured performer. Participating in the opening of the Houston Wortham Theater Center in 1987, the Gilbert & Sullivan Society moved from Jones Hall to that center's more intimate Cullen Theater, better suited to their presentations.

G&S has come a long way since I first worked with them. The troupe competed three times in the Buxton England G & S International Festival and won best of show, best musical director, best stage director, best costumes, best chorus, best female lead and many other awards. Scholarships have increased and winners have gone on to make a name for themselves in the world of opera. Most recently, Sasha Cooke, one of three G & S apprentices who have joined the Metropolitan Opera company, is predicted to become a major star.

G & S opening night parties, hosted by some of Houston's rich and famous, were highlights of their performances. Prominent beer distributor **Frank Horlock** and his wife opened their lavish home for two of those while I worked with the company. Among the many distinguished guests were **J. Howard Marshall** and his tall, slender super-proper, plain looking wife Maizie who served on many civic and cultural committees with me. This was long before Anna Nicole Smith. J. Howard always looked sickly and it seems I remember him in a wheelchair at the time. After Maizie's death, who would ever have guessed that J. Howard would become addicted to "gentlemen's clubs", strippers and lap dancers. And take on sexpot Anna Nicole Smith for his second wife. Maizie has probably revolved in her grave several times.

G&S founder John Cooper continued to be active with the society after he left Kinkaid to open his own John Cooper School in the Woodlands outside of Houston. According to Mary Metz, another founding Gilbert & Sullivan Society member and performer, "We still seem to struggle with our Houston audiences when we do a lesser known piece like *Ruddy Gore*, but we have a duty to educate."

Metz, now 83 and secretary of the G & S Society, received the Member of the Order of the British Empire (MPE) award for her work as a volunteer in Houston and between Houston and Aberdeen Scotland. She was honored with a medal and a Warrant from Queen Elizabeth at Buckingham Palace. She is chairman of the

Houston/ Grampian Association (Scottish Sister International) and has overseen the annual Scottish St. Andrew's Day dinner in Houston for many years.

All "stars" are not performers. Artists, chefs, even every day great people can be included in the galaxy. Gallerie Barbizon opened in the original Town & Country Village in Houston, before it became an enclosed shopping mall, featuring artists from around the world. It was owned and operated by Gustav Alker and his sons, an enterprising Hungarian family who had been European art dealers and wanted to add the European touch to Houston. I was retained to handle the opening and promote incoming artists and exhibits which changed about every six weeks.

Charles Beckendorf, renowned wild life artist, was one of my favorites. He was most popular in Texas and was featured in encore exhibits at Barbizon over a couple of years. A big hulk of a man, his style was beautiful and realistic. He made the usual rounds of interviews with me and gifted me with a series of his special commemorative limited edition Six Big Cats of the World lithographs. A recognized writer and protector of wild life, Beckendorf was the driving force behind the establishment of a national wildlife art museum.

Beckendorf was commissioned to paint a wild life mural for the African Hall at the Museum of Natural Science in Houston'a Hermann Park. He was finishing up on the three year project when I was scheduled to meet him to plan publicity for the opening of the new hall. When I arrived, his ladder, paints and scaffold were all in place in front of the largest painting measuring 13 x 136 feet which he was finishing. But no Beckendorf. Probably at lunch, the staff assumed. The truth, according to his wife who runs the Beckendorf Gallery in Fredericksburg,Texas, "There was a payment dispute and Charles left until it was resolved. He eventually completed the mural."

Charles Beckendorf passed away in 1996, but his wildlife paintings will remain collector items forever.

Lui-sang Wong, well known Chinese watercolor artist, was born in Taisun in Kwangtung, China but moved to San Francisco. Exhibited throughout the U.S. and Asia, two of Wong's paintings were displayed in the Modern Art of Asia museum in Tokyo, Japan. His exhibit at Gallerie Barbazon was popular and we made the usual media interview rounds with an added demonstration at the Houston public library where he completed a beautiful bluebird in a tree with a poem in

Chinese calligraphy in less than an hour. The results of that session now hang on my living room wall.

Wong came to the U.S. In 1961 when he presented one of his paintings, "Attempting to Land on the Moon" in which the eagle symbolizes the conquest of space, to President Kennedy. He went on to exhibit and teach throughout the states and Canada and finally settled in California. His first Gallerie Barbizon exhibit opened in 1974.

Lion guards his Denzel Carousel at Astroworld

LEARNING EXPERIENCE GROUP TOURS!

$1

Each student in groups of 20 or more. One adult FREE with each group of 20.

10% discount for adults in groups of 20 or more.

ALABAMA
COUSHATTA
Activity Schedule

FALL AND SPRING

	Adults	Children
Wednesday thru Friday	$4.50	$2.50
Saturday and Sunday	$5.00	$3.00

Tourist destination: Alabama Coushatta Indian Reservation.

Oil tycoon R. E. Bob Smith and Astrodome partner Judge Roy Hofheinz at the VIP Players Club.

Playboys' Pappy Selph with my mom, Marie Zenzen.

Houston Gilbert & Sullivan Society's founder, advocate and performer John Cooper.

J. Howard Marshall, before Anna Nicole Smith.

Long time G&S supporter and performer Mary Metz is still going strong in her 80s.

Cats, from a collection artist Charles Beckendorf gave, "To my friend, Rita."

CHAPTER 10

Odds & Ends

As a public relations consultant, I was expected to serve the community in a variety of volunteer projects including co-chairman of Houston's Bicentennial celebration and parade with Emil Karam, a city employee. The event involved lots of people and even more politics. Ultimately, we were left with a lot of work and no budget. And not much thanks. It actually became a political challenge, and our Bicentennial Celebration was renamed Summer Festival. An odd choice, we thought.

Focusing on the historic, much neglected Allen's Landing on Buffalo Bayou in downtown where Allen Brothers landed and founded the city of Houston., we decided to have our parade begin and end there, on Main street instead of the usual route ending at what was then Foley's department store at the opposite end of Main. Other activities were scheduled around the downtown area, but we did the first Art & Crafts show at the Landing, the beginning of many.

The building at the Landing had been vacant for quite some time, but after the Summer Festival, renowned sculptor David Addicks opened a trendy club on the top floor featuring laser light shows outside on the weekends. He has become more famous in recent times and his sculptures are all over Houston and Texas as well as around the country. His studio is currently located in an old warehouse district near the downtown area.

Making Allen's Landing presentable for a celebration was another matter. Decaying buildings and a mom-and-pop gas station eyesore dominated the scene. The adjacent Buffalo Bayou had not developed as hoped and the only new addition to the area was the Continental Houston hotel which was built across from the Landing in early 1970.

After much pleading, I managed to get then **Mayor Louis Welch** to agree to demolish the gas station and move "mom and pop" to another location. That was a promising beginning.

Putting a parade together is a full time-plus job from the logistics of participant placement to getting a noteworthy parade marshal who would bring people down to "that part of town". Our first choice was country music singer Mickey Gilley who had gained fame as the owner/operator of his namesake Gillly's honky tonk located in Pasadena outside of Houston. It became even more famous as the location for most of the action in John Travolta's movie *Urban Cowboy*.

Because of a previous commitment, Gilley couldn't make it. And, without a budget and only the offer of free rooms and food from the Continental Houston, not too many stars were interested.

Karam came up with the idea of the **Staple Singers** a hep gospel group who were superstars almost everywhere, except in Houston, Texas. We contacted them and Pop Staples agreed that it would be an interesting gig and since they had no conflict, they would be happy to participate. It was probably not their most exciting booking, but it was different and relaxing.

We decided to have an arts and crafts show at Allen's Landing during the celebration with fireworks scheduled at the stroke of midnight on July 4, shot off from across the Landing. Getting everything in place required lots of scurrying back and forth over busy streets. Always the klutz, I stumbled on one of those trips and shattered my elbow. Model and really good person

Katherine Blissard came to my rescue. She picked me up and got me to a downtown hospital. I checked myself out the next morning. I had things to do.

Models and fashion shows were big time during the 70s in Houston with agent Barry Horn booking most of them for an agency, Ben something. Elsa Rosborough, who taught grooming and modeling at the University of Houston, was an internationally known model and trained her students to walk and pose, including my daughter, Viki. Elsa is no longer with us, but some of the other models are. Blissard is a writer for "H" magazine, Houston's society sheet, and popular Warner Roberts has a regular column in that paper.

Bubbly red-haired Dallas Hill, mother of five (I think) had bigger aspirations than walking the runway. She wanted to be a star performer. She put a band together, Dallas and the Cowboys (after the football team), and I managed to get them booked at the Marriott for a couple of weekends. Her signature song was PERSONALITY! The band played and sang the verse and when the chorus started..."she's got ..." Dallas belted out in her best and loudest voice...PERSONALITY! Some of her friends came to check out her debut, but the rest of the gig was a bust. Don't think Dallas ever made the big time singing.

Loaded up on the makeshift float, the Staple Singers made the trail down Main Street and participated in the opening gala at the Continental Houston saluting the Daughters of the Republic of Texas. They probably enjoyed not being noticed. Or maybe not.

In addition to the crafts and art show at the Landing prior to the fireworks, entertainment was staged from a loading platform on a historic building on the opposite side of the Bayou. A first for Houston.

Karam came up with the idea of us taking over the beer concession to get a little monetory reward for our time and efforts. It paid off. We each wound up with over a thousand dollars in profits. I did not know about his scheme until he presented me with a check. What a nice surprise.

Local musical groups like Greg Harbor and the Gypsies, the **Patsy Swayze** Jazz Ballet Company and the **Over the Hill Gang** Jazz and Banjo Band, who were regulars at Joe Huber's Seafood Restaurant on Market Square, were among the featured entertainment. They all played banjos. My children and I joined them on a junket to Eureka Springs, Arkansas for a banjo competition. I owned a house there. It was robbed, the hot tub stolen. I sold it.

Patrick Swayze was a dedicated young dancer who performed with his mother's jazz ballet company. Still In his teens he joined a tour with the Disney on Parade Ice Show. Upon returning home to his four brothers and sisters and his mom's dance studio, he became smitten with one of his mother's students, sixteen year old Lisa Niemi. After graduating from high school, she followed Patrick to New York where they joined the New York City Ballet.

The couple married on June 12, 1975. Swayze credits his wife with helping him conquer many of his demons and insecurities over the past thirty years. Patrick is currently fighting one of his scarriest battles with pancreatic cancer. As of this writing, he's winning.

When Patrick went to Hollywood to make movie, mom Patsy followed, opened a dance studio in Simi, California and became a popular choreographer working on several movies including Urban Cowboy. She later married musician Ray Rogers and is currently a part of the Silver Foxes, making personal appearances at retirement centers, encouraging activity at any age.

Patrick Swayze succumbed to pancreatic cancer in 2009.

Highlight of that Houston Bicentennial evening was the midnight fireworks display. We paid for them by selling some old park benches which the Houston Parks Department upgraded. We added the name of the donor on a plaque attached to the back. They were placed all around the city, But they were rather fragile and have long since disappeared.

The fireworks were spectacular. They were coordinated with a Houston Symphony rendition of the Star Spangled Banner with Houston vocalist June Terry bringing tears to those in the audience. She played Miss Mona in Houston's pre-broadway production of the Best Little Whorehouse in Texas, which also included Marvin Zindler. He played himself, a brash television reporter.

Crown jewel in our Bicentennial entertainment lineup was jazz great **Arnett Cobb.** Labeled "Wild Man of the Tenor Sax" he shared a Grammy award with B. B. King in 1984 for best traditional blues performance "Blues n' Jazz," MCA. A serious illness brought Cobb back to Houston after touring the world as a replacement for Illinois Jacquet with Lionel Hampton's band for several years. He then formed his own seven piece group, but his ongoing success was interrupted by a 1956 car crash which put him on crutches.

His father, also a musician, had written a song exalting the city of Houston which he felt would be most appropriate for the Bicentennial. It had never been played in public before.

When I met him, he was teaching music and coached Kashmere's Black Rain student jazz band with music director Conrad Johnson which played the Bicentennial and after, competed in Japan. Today, they are the Kashmere Reunion Band

Cobb continued to perform as a soloist through the 1970s and '80s. In 1986, he founded the Jazz Heritage Society of Texas which established the Texas Jazz Archives at the Houston Public Library.

Although I knew he was great, I was not really aware of how great Arnett Cobb really was until after his death in 1989. Born in Houston's poorest Fourth Ward district, he never forgot his old neighborhood or Wheatley, his old high school. Arnett Cobb was and always will be an inspiration to his people, the city of Houston and to jazz musicians and enthusiasts around the world.

All in all, that Houston bicentennial (Summer Festival) was a huge success and was the beginning of an annual Summer Fest and increased interest in the Allen's Landing area with the opening of the University of Houston's downtown campus and the clean up and/or demolition of some of Houston's most historic structures.

Attempting to attract attention to the area, I opened a restaurant in one of the threatened structures which served only on Fridays. I prepared the food myself, and set it up outside for a full bayou view. Maybe I inspired internationally known sculptor David Addicks to open his laser light club in that spot.

Houston has never seemed partial to historical structures. When the Rice Hotel received its historical designation protecting it from demolition, Mayor Louis Welch wryly commented, "Guess somebody has to like early ugly!" And, as the late Chronicle society editor Betty Ewing recalled, while at a dinner at the Queen's palace in London, Mayor Welch was asked if there was anything like it in Houston?" His reply, according to Betty was, "No, but we could always build it."

Probably that's why almost every time Houston artist **Steve Besselman** created an awesome rendition of a notable historic building, it was the kiss of death for it. Within weeks of the drawing, the building disappeared. Like the Pink Pussy Cat exotic dancers club housed in a late 1800's treasure and the Wig Shop, down the street.

When asked why the demolitions were ordered, the city fathers shrugged, "We must have gotten the wrong address." or "We didn't know it was historic."

Besselman continued to sketch buildings around Houston's historic Old Market Square until his death. But his legend lives on in a lower level downtown Houston gallery run by one of his former partners.

One of those buildings was the Kennedy Bakery connected to the Kennedy Trading Post which served the military in the mid to late 1800s and converted to office, retail and eateries in the early 1900s. Located across from Old Market Square, a brick arch connected it to the current bakery occupant, La Carafe, reputed to be the oldest bar in Houston and a real tourist attraction.

Arriving in the middle of the night, the demolition crew was stopped from destroying the arch by the owner of Warren's Inn, a still popular bar on an opposite street. At the time, I was working with architect **Robert "Bob" Timme** who was designing a four-story garden home for me in Houston's trendy Montrose area. He was also teaching at Rice University and University of Houston while a partner in Architects in Cahoots, later changed to Taft Architects for a more dignified image.

At the University of Houston, Timme was working with an exchange professor from Italy who specialized in restorations. He agreed to take the Kennedy Bakery project on and the arch was reconstructed by students under his and Timme's guidance. Today, La Carafe still stands, but part of the Kennedy Trading Post and the arch were not that lucky.

The "Montrose Treehouse" that Timme designed for me in 1978 was featured in magazines all over the world because of its unique compatibility with the older homes in the area and brought Taft Architects (they were located on Taft Street) lots of new business The redesign of the YMCA on Waugh Drive near downtown Houston followed and the group gained an international reputation for their creativity and sensitivity. Timme moved to California in the 1990s as dean of architecture for University of Southern Califonia. He passed away of cancer a few years ago.

After the Bicentennial, I volunteered to help Patsy Swayze with publicity on her reviews which were held at Miller Theater in Houston's Hermann Park. The shows were a family affair with Patrick and his brothers and sisters performing with the troupe and his late father setting up and taking down the scenery and hauling the costumes. One of the featured dancers, who shall remain nameless, became a friend who later helped himself to what little jewelry I had. He called to sympathize with me because I had been robbed. I was not aware of it until he told me.

Ballet has always been one of my passions as a spectator, not a performer, which is why I also volunteered to work with Emma Mae Horn, a former dancer and director of an elite school of ballet in Houston. We moved her showcase recitals from small rehearsal stages to Jones Hall, bringing increased interest and donations to the company.

One of her earlier pupils was **Andrea Vodenhal** who went on to New York and later joined the Washington, D.C. ballet where she met her husband (no longer) **Eugene Collins**, an outstanding dancer who grew up on the streets of New York and proved that tough guys could be respected ballet dancers. His technique brought a raw revitalized energy to performances.

The pair came to Houston as featured dancers with the Houston ballet until Eugene left. Andrea remained a lead dancer until she retired a few years ago.

Disease of the Month was another part of my volunteer work. Heart, cystic fibrosis and cancer were my main thrusts. Working with Mary Lou King, publicity director for the American Cancer Society in Houston, I became the state coordinator for publicity and got to work with **Lawrence Welk** and Grand Ole Opry's **Minnie Pearl** when they were featured at a local cancer fund raiser. They were both wonderful and put me back in touch with the star lights that I had been used to.

In 1994, second husband and my most enthusiastic supporter Thomas Edward Heck of Berlin, Germany and I decided to build a house near downtown San Antonio. The living is easy but strippers, stars and presidents are practically nil. The closest I come to stars these days is as a volunteer usher at the Majestic Theater. I remember when Sid Schlenker, Allen Becker and I toured the theater while it was being refurbished. Pace Management was going to handle the bookings when it reopened. That was a very long time ago.

I was incredibly blessed to grow up at a time when really neat creative job opportunities were available to anyone who could handle them. Being a female, being young, not having a degree didn't seem to matter. The bottom line was: "can you produce the results we need?"

In tune with the times, the environment has become my "star" attraction. As The Green Connection, I have written a column for the local daily newspaper, host-produce a television show and published a magazine *Product & Design/The Green Connection,* covering green building, energy saving and sustainable living. Also produce the Green Connection television program which has been running since 1995 on a local community channel.

My most recent star attraction was Dr. William C. Davis, a remarkable man fighting to put renewable energies at the head of the class in his Natural Sciences Department at St. Philip's College in San Antonio. Through his chemistry expertise, he created the formula for one of America's most popular comfort foods, instant mashed potatoes.

He was studying potatoes at the University of Idaho to develop an instant cube potato for Lipton's Soups when his failure turned into instant mashed potatoes. He has several patents for everything from glue to purified water which he developed for Coca Cola. Soft serve ice cream was another of his projects.

His brother, beloved actor/writer/director Ossie Davis was his best friend. As a student, Dr. Davis joined his brother in New York and became chummy with lots of movie stars incuding Paul Newman and, of course, his sister-in-law, Ruby Dee.

In 2003, I developed and coordinated an international Fuel Cell Literacy Conference for St. Philip's College. I'm not a tree hugger, but unless the world addresses the pollution/global warming issues, we won't be seeing any of the true stars, the ones in the heavens above. They will be hidden by polluted air from fuel fumes and undisciplined energy usage.

That same year, I was fortunate to introduce renowned Asian artist Yi Z, an art professor at the University of Hainan, to Texas. Coordinating gallery exhibits for him in San Antonio, Austin, Houston and Corpus Christi, I was overwhelmed by his unique talent. Although he covered a broad range of subjects, his forte' was creating eloquent paintings to illustrate poems in ancient literature.

A member of the Chinese Fine Art Association, he is represented in the U.S. by Lotus Gallery in Austin.

Now, being faced with energy shortages, pollution and global warming scares, I have always claimed to not be a tree hugger, but for the time I have left, I would like to influence change in daily living by spreading the word on green technology and living. At the rate the world is going, change is an overwhelming challenge. But not nearly so much fun as...

Strippers, Stars & Presidents!

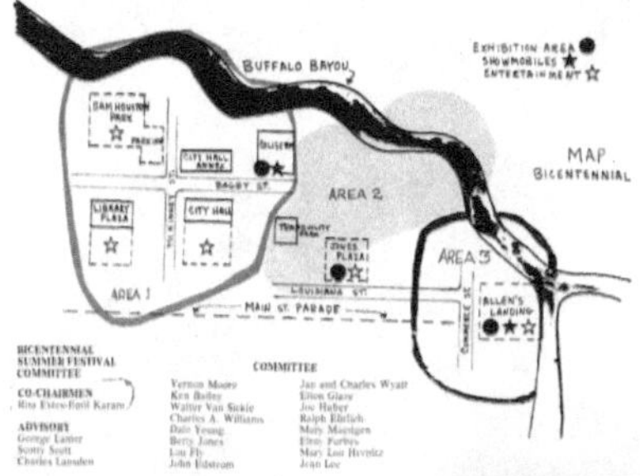

Allen's Landing
Jones Plaza
City Hall Annex
Music Hall Annex
Library Plaza
Sam Houston Park
City Hall Complex

Houston Bicentennial Celebration.program.

Co-chairman Emil Karam and I cut the Celebration cake in front of the late Contental Houston, Bicentennial headquarters.

Schedule

JULY 2 — FRIDAY

FLAG CEREMONY AND PATRIOTIC CONCERT. Noon - 1 pm. Allens Landing.
Raising of Texas flag by Texas Army. Presentation of the Six Flags over Texas. Patriotic concert. Festival kickoff address. Salute to Space, address by Louie Welch. Buffalo Bayou Fountain dedication.

HOUSTON SYMPHONY. 8 p.m. Jones Hall.
Compositions by Schuman, Dvorak, and Samuel Barber. "Old American Songs by Aaron Copland with Allen Baker baritone soloist. Murry Sidlin, guest conductor.

VAUDEVILLE SHOW. 8-10 p.m. Allen's Landing Barge.
Capt. Harold Gunn of Ch. 20 emcees variety acts including the Over the Hill Gang band, Bicentennial Tippy Tappers, Jana Stewart, and others.

FIRST ANNUAL LIBERTY BELLE MASQUERADE BALL. 9:30 p.m. - 2 a.m. Ramada Inn - Allen's Landing - Ballroom and Poolside.
Gala Ball with the Houston Liberty Belles as hostesses. Special Bicentennial fashion show. Jerry Dale, emcee. Open to the public. $5 cash bar. Three bands will play.

BAYOU CLARIFICATION DEMONSTRATION. Buffalo Bayou from Shepherd Dr. to Allen's Landing.
American Institute of Chemical Engineers demonstrate water clarification. (July 2, 3, and 4.)

SPACE EXHIBITS. 1-5 p.m. Albert Thomas Space Hall of Fame. (July 1, 2, 3, and 4.)

HOUSTON POST SPRING ART SHOW. Ramada Inn - Allen's Landing - Lobby. (July 2, 3, and 4)

YOUTH FAIR ART EXHIBIT. Noon-5 p.m. Houston Natural Gas Corp. Lobby.

PHOTO EXHIBIT. Alley Theatre. 10 a.m. thru showtime (July 1-3). **6 p.m.- showtime** (July 4). Exhibit — Reflections of the Alley. Photographic collection of past productions and the after portraits by Kaye Marvins.

JULY 3 — SATURDAY

BICENTENNIAL PARADE. 10 a.m. Main Street from Dallas St. to Allen's Landing.
Theme: Houston You're A Grand Old Town. Features floats and music depicting America and Houston—past, present, future. Guests: The Staple Singers and Tom Poston. "Duckie," KRLY & Frank Haley KTRH, commentate.

BICENTENNIAL FLOTILLA. 2 p.m. Buffalo Bayou at Allen's Landing.
Sixty decorated boats sail from Kemah to salute the Bicentennial. Co-sponsored by the Rendezvous Festival, Houston Power Squadron and Galveston Power Squadron. Bob Stevenson, KXYZ, commentator.

MUNICIPAL BAND CONCERT. 3:30 p.m. Allen's Landing.
Top 40 music.

LIBRARY PLAZA. Noon - 5 p.m. Bagby at Walker.
Music, exhibits, arts and crafts, antique car exhibits.

HISTORIC HOMES TOURS. 1-4:30 p.m. Sam Houston Park.

INTERNATIONAL FESTIVAL. Noon to dusk. Jones Plaza, Music Hall Annex, Allen's Landing.
Arts, crafts, food and entertainment from nations around the world.

AMERICANA FESTIVAL. Noon to dusk. City Hall Annex, Sam Houston Park, Allen's Landing.
Select antique show, arts and crafts, entertainment, kiddie rides, pony rides, games and contests, all dealing with Houston's historical past.

STANDING ARTISTS SHOW. Noon-8 p.m. Alley Theatre-Jones Hall area.

TABLE GAMES. Noon to 6 p.m. City Hall Reflection Pool, Tranquility Park.
Checkers, chess, backgammon and a variety of quiet games sponsored by the Houston Parks and Recreation Dept.

CANOE RENTAL. Noon to dusk. Allen's Landing.
Sponsored by Boy Scouts.

NEW GAMES. Noon-5 p.m. Tranquility Park.

YOUTH FAIR ART EXHIBIT. Noon-5 p.m. Houston Natural Gas Corp. Lobby.

CARNIVAL. Open at noon. Bagby at McKinney.
Rides, games, food and entertainment.

BICENTENNIAL PATRIOTIC EXTRAVAGANZA. 8 - midnite. Allen's Landing.
Ron Stone of Ch. 2 hosts a variety show featuring music of days gone by. Includes a special concert by the Houston Civic Symphony and special guest June Terry.

FIREWORKS SPECTACULAR. Midnite. Allen's Landing.
A fantastic patriotic display by famous fireworks designer Al Cohen.

JULY 4 — SUNDAY

BELL RINGING CEREMONY. 1 p.m. Entire City.
St. John's Church in Sam Houston Park will lead the ceremony involving practically every church in Houston. Coordinated by the Boy Scouts to coincide with the national bell-ringing ceremony.

MUNICIPAL BAND CONCERT. 2 p.m. Sam Houston Park Gazebo.
Bert Roth, director. 25-piece municipal band.

TOASTMASTERS. Noon-4 p.m. Library Plaza, Allen's Landing.
"Get It Off Your Chest." Public invited to talk on various current topics, with prizes for best discussion.

HISTORIC HOMES TOURS. 2-4:30 p.m. Sam Houston Park.

INTERNATIONAL FESTIVAL. Noon to dusk. Jones Plaza, Allen's Landing, Music Hall Annex.

AMERICANA FESTIVAL. Noon to dusk. City Hall Annex, Sam Houston Park, Allen's Landing.

STANDING ARTISTS SHOW. noon-8 p.m. Alley Theater-Jones Hall area.

TABLE GAMES. Noon to 6 p.m. City Hall Reflection Pond, Tranquility Park.

NEW GAMES. Noon-5 p.m. Tranquility Park.

DOWNTOWN BUILDING TOUR. 2 p.m.-5 p.m. Downtown Houston.
Old Cotton Exchange Building, 900 Commerce Street Building, Jones Hall, Alley Theatre.

CONTEMPORARY JAZZ CONCERT. 4 to 7 p.m. Allen's Landing.
The New Jazz Ensemble, Bevianna and Strings & Things and others.

TWO HUNDRED YEARS WITH LOVE. 4-8p.m. Marriott Hotel.
Original musical show by Temple Emanu El. Special "Melting Pot" buffet. Cash food and bar. Admission free. 723-7299.

Free Houtran MiniBus Shuttle Service -

JULY 2 & 3
FROM NOON TIL 6 P.M.

Free Parking -
One Allen
Center Garage

A SPECIAL THANKS TO:
National Standard Bank
Ramada Inn-Civic Center
Houston Parks and Recreation Dept.
The Beasley Printing Co.
Anderson Plastics
Harris County
Bowser Bros.
Houston Post
Houston Chronicle
Maria Shelton
Festival Productions
Dino & Joe San Tangelo
Evelyn Chitwood
Kaylyn Hall
Helene Stanilla
Don Hicks
Paige Haines
The Lamb
Ron Orur & Assoc.
Skyscraper Adv.
Houston Terminal Warehouse
Freeman Decorating
Texas Educational Aids
Port of Houston
Simmon Florist
J. Michael Sorg
Hooks-Epstein Gallery
Temple Emanu El
Ed Adams
Lisa Ellis
Windmill Dinner Theatre
John Silva
Jewell Jackson
Bob Brewer
Judge Joe Lindsey
Jim Shane
ALL RADIO & TELEVISION STATIONS
ALL MAGAZINES

Happenings at the Bicentennial Celebration.

The Bicentennial medal artwork coordinated by Hooks-Epstein Gallery owner Gerry Hooks.

Bayou Banjo club members and I inspect an ode at the factory on the way to Eureka Springs, Arkansas for a banjo festival.

A Steve Besselman drawing of an historical buildingnear Market Square.

La Carafe, Houston's oldest bar next to the demolished Kennedy Trading Post.

Jazz great Arnett Cobb coached Kashmere high school's Black Rain jazz band for a Houston Bicentennial performance and international competitions.

The Houston Post 1C

ate here

OUR FRIDAY photo stars are ASA award-winning Taft Architects owner **Bob Timme,** ad agency chief **Rita Estes** and **Saied Hakimzadeh,** owner of the increasingly popular saloon and cafe, Baba Yega. Bob and Rita meet often at the Baba Yega to huddle on the progress of the townhouse treehouse Bob has designed and is building for Rita on her Fairview property in the Montrose section. It soars 'waaay up there, four stories, and when she moves in about Thanksgiving, she'll rank as the street's No. 1 High Living resident. Rita commissioned Bob to design her something special, and he really has. He joined the new treehouse on to her exisiting home and office and Rita says the view from the top is really something, especially the panoramic look toward downtown.

MOVERS AND SHAKERS — The Hyatt Regency's **Jo Ann Craplitz** says the hotel's Crystal Forest is expecting great biz for the Sept. 26-Oct. 15 appearance of singer **Bill Nash.** He'll be backed by the **Bayou Family.** ★ Get ready for the great Sunday eve party launching The Great Caruso, the newest restaurant in the ever-growing chain of **Toni Renee, Ernie** and **Spiro Criezis.** Those who've peeked are raving about the club's decor. The word is there is nothing like it anywhere around. Toni's sister **Jerry Sisman** has jetted in from London for the opening doings.

Bob, Rita and Saied

— Post photo by Manuel Chavez

Architect, the late Bob Timme, me and Said Haskimzaden, Baba Yega owner

San Antonio's HemisFair, 35 years later.

Showing Hap Garman's Summer Fest poster to Mayor Louie Welch and Parks and Recreation director.

Patrick and Patsy (mother) Swayze.

Daughters of the Republic of Texas aboard the Sam Houston barge.

YiZ exhibit invitation.

Hap Garman interpreted Foley's Thanksgiving Day Parade, 1981.

Ossie Davis with brothers William and Kenneth celebrate Mom's 95th birthday.

Dr. William C. Davis, a man of the future.

Me and The Green Connection...for a more sustainable world.

Socialite and the basis for the movie Charlie Wilson's War starring Julia Roberts, Joanne King poses with the Bushes: Presidents George H.W. and George and Governor Jeb. She's still a beauty in her 80s.

ACKNOWLEDGEMENTS

Although most of the content of this book is based on my memories and photos, I had to do some followup on the "characters" to bring them up to date... to find out if they were even still here. Following are the sources for this research. If anyone has been overlooked, it is totally unintentional. Please accept my apologies and thank you for your understanding. If you contact me, I will be sure to include you in an updated version of Strippers Stars & Presidents. Most of my "contacts" were internet websites with no phone or other contact information available.

Doug Moe, Madison Capital Times;
musicbase.h1.ru/PPB/ppb13/bio.1382.htm;
www/rayteam,com/1947.html;
www.classicmoviemusicals.com/dr1.htm;
www.chicaago.urban-history.org/sites/theaters/chicago.htm;
wikipedia .org,
reuters.com;
www.elvisly-yours.com/aldvorin1.shtml;
jane-addams-hull-house-museum.visit-chicago-illinois.com/;
www.yelp.com/biz_photos/oxA7dliKBg7dt6t6blQ?selec;
www.compassrose.org/balaban-and-katz/Oriental-Theatre.htm;
www.chiippbulib.org/008subject/001artmusic/muggsy/msphotos;
www.nextshow.biz/ebonjabio.html;
home.flash.net/-mrradio/album.htm; home.comcast.net/-gecadero/eddyarnold.htm; MPTV.net;
www.uiaa.org/chicaago/highlights/images/40th_navypier.jpg;
www.loc.gov/exhibits/bobhope/images/vevg2.jpg;
www.hogansheroesfanclub.com/castHovisLarry.php;
www.teddwebb.com/legends/col_atom_parker.html;
Academic Planet.com;
www.celebhost.net/tommysands/bio.html;
www.rockabillyhall.com/tommysands.html;
George H. W. Bush, Academy of Achievement, a Museum of Living History;
www/rootsweb.com/-txnavarr/obituaries/pg90059.htm;
www.jacksonskates.com/photos/pics/T-19jpg

www.apartacus.schoolnet.co.uk/jfkbushG.htm;
www.bobdelmonteque.com/;
www.crimelibrary.com/notorious_murders/family/jacques_mos;
Maxine Harris,Houston Chronicle, December 28, 1997;
www.geocities.com/murder_stories3/minns3.html;
http://spring.net/yapp-bin/public/read/tv69
http://main.wgbh.org/wgbh/NTW/FA/TITLES/melanie323.html;
http://www.aimpress.com/minnsbio.htm;
http://cbass.com/faq(4).htm;
Bryan Stankiewicz, Chamber of Commerce, Hawaii; Native Hawaiian Chamber of Commerce,
George Vincent; Mike Matey, Surfline;
Legendary Surfers, by Malcolm Gault-Williams;
www.legendarysurfers.com/sur/legends/lsc302_strauch.html;
www.extremehorizon.com/surfhistory.asp;
www.dickweekley.org/weekley/011101.asp;
www.haaf.org/en/art/?128;
www.abpeople.com///abpeple/docs/brewerys/houstoh/houston;
www.tsha.utexas.edu/handbook/online/articles/CC.hjc23.html;
karws.gso.uri.edu/marsh/jfk-conspiracy/connally.htm;

DEDICATION

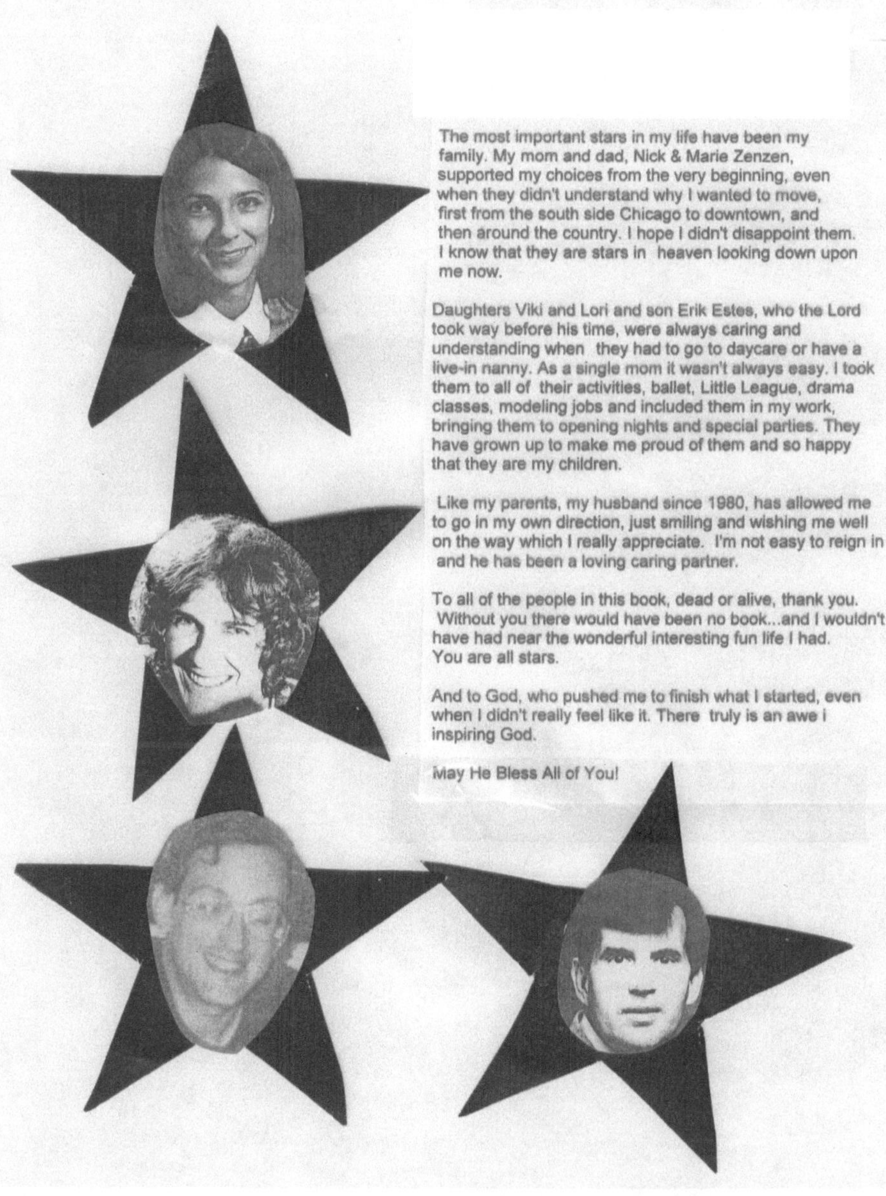

The most important stars in my life have been my family. My mom and dad, Nick & Marie Zenzen, supported my choices from the very beginning, even when they didn't understand why I wanted to move, first from the south side Chicago to downtown, and then around the country. I hope I didn't disappoint them. I know that they are stars in heaven looking down upon me now.

Daughters Viki and Lori and son Erik Estes, who the Lord took way before his time, were always caring and understanding when they had to go to daycare or have a live-in nanny. As a single mom it wasn't always easy. I took them to all of their activities, ballet, Little League, drama classes, modeling jobs and included them in my work, bringing them to opening nights and special parties. They have grown up to make me proud of them and so happy that they are my children.

Like my parents, my husband since 1980, has allowed me to go in my own direction, just smiling and wishing me well on the way which I really appreciate. I'm not easy to reign in and he has been a loving caring partner.

To all of the people in this book, dead or alive, thank you. Without you there would have been no book...and I wouldn't have had near the wonderful interesting fun life I had. You are all stars.

And to God, who pushed me to finish what I started, even when I didn't really feel like it. There truly is an awe i inspiring God.

May He Bless All of You!

www.ingramcontent.com/pod-product-compliance
Lightning Source LLC
LaVergne TN
LVHW091036080826
845145LV00002B/517
* 9 7 8 0 6 1 5 2 4 8 9 0 5 *